Implementing a Data Warehouse:
A methodology that worked

Bruce R. Ullrey, MS, CIO
Rumpke Consolidated Companies

AuthorHouse™
1663 Liberty Drive,
Suite 200
Bloomington, IN 47403
www.authorhouse.com
Phone: 1-800-839-8640

AuthorHouse™ UK Ltd.
500 Avebury Boulevard
Central Milton Keynes,
MK9 2BE
www.authorhouse.co.uk
Phone: 08001974150

First published by AuthorHouse 3/16/2007

ISBN: 978-1-4259-9167-8 (sc)

Printed in the United States of America
Bloomington, Indiana

This book is printed on acid-free paper.

Acknowledgements

An effort the size of our data warehouse implementation requires a team.

I want to first thank Janet Goudy for her clear thinking, her tenacious adherence to the vision of what our company needed, and her patience with me when I didn't understand how the company really worked. Next, I want to thank Bill Langston and Mary Lynn Treadwell for their encouragement when I wondered if and why I should document our journey to success.

Thanks also to the Rumpke staff and managers who were very patient with the data warehouse implementation when I wanted to over-engineer and became a little too "fire, ready, aim" with the project.

And finally, I want to thank Phil Wehrman for trusting enough to let the project happen.

Table of Contents

Step 10: Deploy the Data Warehouse 147

Step 11: Begin Data Warehouse Support 155

Develop Measures of Success 156

Appendices

Glossary 203

Recommended Reading 207

Bibliography 208

A Graphic of the Methodology

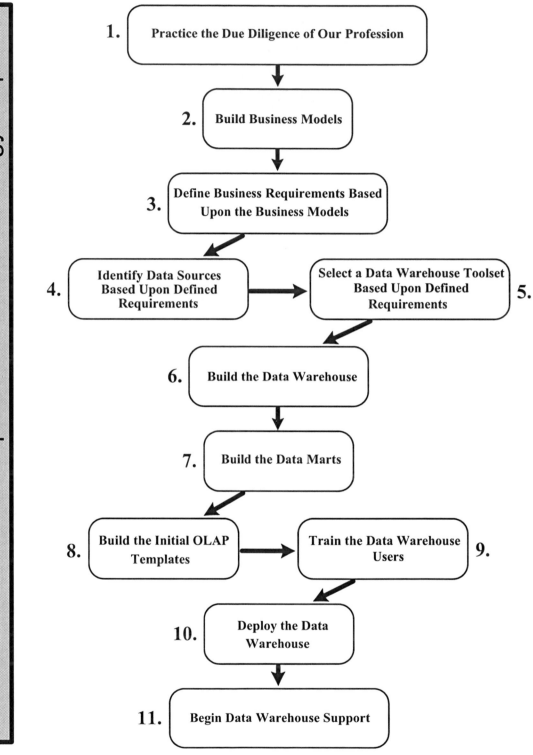

<< Data Warehouse Implementation Methodology Steps >>

1. Practice the Due Diligence of Our Profession

2. Build Business Models

3. Define Business Requirements Based Upon the Business Models

4. Identify Data Sources Based Upon Defined Requirements

5. Select a Data Warehouse Toolset Based Upon Defined Requirements

6. Build the Data Warehouse

7. Build the Data Marts

8. Build the Initial OLAP Templates

9. Train the Data Warehouse Users

10. Deploy the Data Warehouse

11. Begin Data Warehouse Support

> **"The only way of discovering the limits
> of the possible is to venture a little ways
> past them into the impossible."**
> *Arthur C. Clark*

Executive Overview

The perceived difficulty of implementing a data warehouse and developing the associated business intelligence has reached urban myth status. The purpose of this material is to present a practical (and proven) methodology that can be used by computer professionals or business analysts to dispel that myth and successfully implement a small- to medium-sized data warehouse.

Most seasoned business computer professionals already have the majority of the skills necessary to implement an efficient and effective data warehouse and business intelligence system. They just need a jump start to get organized. This document will present that jump start – methodology steps that successfully brought a data warehouse and associated business intelligence to a $350,000,000 regional services company in about a year.

The methodology is generally linear. It begins with applying Systems Development Life Cycle (SDLC) and project management disciplines and moves through building business models, defining business requirements (measurement metrics), sourcing the data, purchasing and installing a data warehouse toolset, building the data warehouse, building data marts, building initial OLAP templates, training users, deploying the toolset, and providing user support. The 11 steps lay out a clear path for development, implementation, and support of a data warehouse and associated business intelligence system.

The purpose of a data warehouse is to provide a place where people can access their data easily. The following diagram illustrates an example of what is typically needed – measuring multiple lines of business within multiple markets across multiple periods of time.

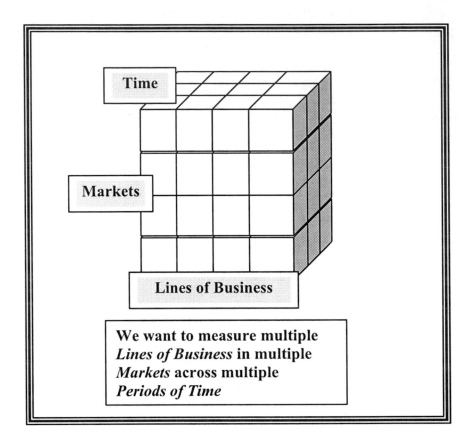

A properly constructed data warehouse, coupled with the associated online analytical processing (OLAP) engine, can provide a two-dimensional view as well as the three-dimensional view depicted in the above model. If constructed well, the data warehouse can become a strategic, tactical, and operational business analysis and planning tool.

This material does not purport to teach data warehousing science. It merely presents the sequence of work to successfully implement the data warehouse currently used at my company. We learned many lessons along the way, and by sharing what we learned, perhaps we can ease the pain of the journey for the next traveler.

Implementation Methodology Overview

Step 1. Practice the due diligence of our profession!

Our business partners in the academic and software provisioning communities have given us a set of tools to perform the due diligence of our profession. We need to use these tools. A number of tools are essential for our purposes here:

- System Development Life Cycle Methodology (SDLC)
- Statement of Work (SOW)
- Request for Proposal (RFP)
- Formal Method of Project Management

Step 2. Build business models

A building is not constructed without a blueprint for the builder to follow. Similarly, business and methodology models are the beginnings of the blueprint for a data warehouse. Different types of models are useful. These models depict areas such as operational processes, management levels, software interfaces, and data file key relationships.

Step 3. Define business requirements based upon the business models

It is essential that business performance metrics be documented and available. KPIs (Key Performance Indicators) and CSFs (Critical Success Factors) used to monitor business performance must be provided to data warehouse developers. A primary goal of the data warehouse is to present the KPIs and CSFs to data warehouse users.

Step 4. Identify data sources based upon defined requirements

Essential questions must be answered. For example:

- Where does raw data that will be used in the data warehouse reside?
- What raw data is necessary to generate required derived data?

Analysis of the lowest level of data available in each system is required to answer these questions.

Step 5. Select a data warehouse toolset based upon defined requirements

Once functional requirements are documented, we will need to find and install a data warehouse and business intelligence toolset that is appropriate for our business. Using the work tools defined in step 1, we will organize our requirements and start our search for the correct vendor.

Step 6. Build the data warehouse

The work of designing and building the physical data warehouse is generally divided into three categories: COPY (sometimes called Extract), BUILD (sometimes called Transform), and LOAD. These general categories will define the following:

- Data to be selected for the data warehouse
- Processes to prepare selected data
- Processes to build files for the data warehouse
- Processes to allow data warehouse users to extract and view information

Step 7. Build the data marts

Data marts contain subsets of data warehouse information. These data subsets are usually developed for specific data warehouse users – for example, Operations, Finance, and Human Resources – or any other specific departmental needs. Data marts eliminate the need for users to access the entire data warehouse when all they want to see is their own information.

Step 8. Build the initial OLAP templates

Online Analytical Processor (OLAP) templates provide views into a data warehouse and data marts. These templates allow users to select and filter information within the data warehouse. Data warehouse developers provide initial OLAP templates.

Step 9. Train the data warehouse users

It isn't enough to develop an innovative and robust data warehouse. Success with the data warehouse is measured by use, not by technical prowess! Users need to be trained and trained and trained….

Step 10. Deploy the data warehouse

Data warehouse deployment is both a functional and political issue. Which users will have what access to the data warehouse? What security will be in place? Is the infrastructure prepared for deployment? Do users have the correct workstation hardware?

Step 11. Begin data warehouse support

Poor post deployment support will cause the implementation to fail. Period.

Defining the steps of this methodology is the purpose of this book. Beginning with Step 2, the reader is shown actual examples from my implementation experience. Examples are drawn from INFINIUM and SoftPak software packages. Some steps include references to materials found helpful as I moved through data warehouse implementation.

A bibliography and glossary are provided.

Encouragement

The benefits of data warehousing to business are proven and demonstrable. The purpose of the material presented here is NOT to build a business case for data warehousing. Nor does this material review and restate data warehousing science. The primary purpose for this material is to provide a body of work describing HOW to actually implement a data warehouse. Many works exist describing the who, what, when, where, and why of data warehousing and business intelligence. These works run the spectrum from *Data Warehousing for Dummies* by Alan J. Simon to a *Data Warehouse Management Handbook* prepared by Richard Kachur. The handbook by Kachur is an excellent work providing the reader with a thorough grounding in the fundamentals of data warehousing management. The most comprehensive presentation of data warehousing art and science is presented in *Data Warehouse Lifecycle Toolkit: Expert Methods for Designing, Developing, and Deploying Data Warehouses* written by Dr. Ralph Kimball et. al. In fact, read anything and everything written by Dr. Ralph Kimbell, Gloria Imhoff, and Bill Inmon. They are the data warehousing leaders and visionaries.

The bookstore at DMReview.com lists over 70 books in the DW Design and Methodology section. A number of them provide excellent reference material. The material presented here supplements these works by joining academic understanding with practical, proven application – lessons learned and all! Start small and establish early success. Arthur C. Clark was right. Venture forward into the (perceived) impossible. You will be amazed at what can be done! Good luck….

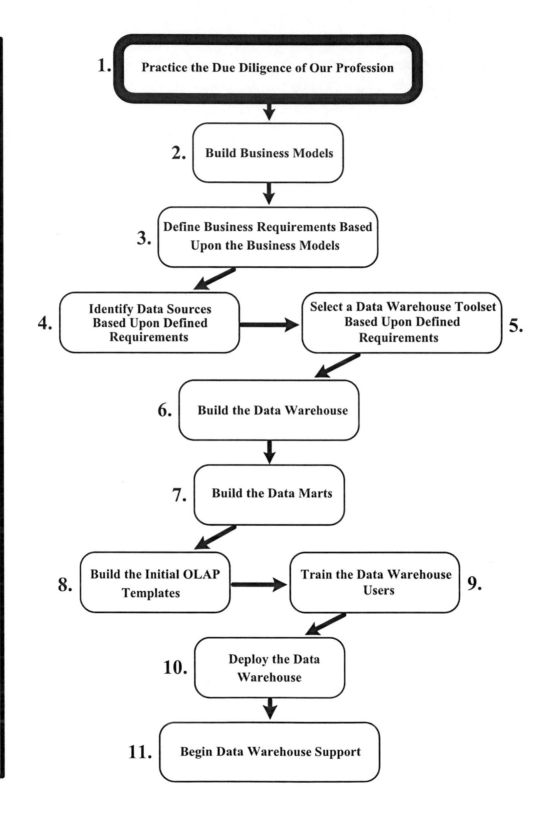

<< Data Warehouse Implementation Methodology Steps >>

1. **Practice the Due Diligence of Our Profession**

2. **Build Business Models**

3. **Define Business Requirements Based Upon the Business Models**

4. **Identify Data Sources Based Upon Defined Requirements**

5. **Select a Data Warehouse Toolset Based Upon Defined Requirements**

6. **Build the Data Warehouse**

7. **Build the Data Marts**

8. **Build the Initial OLAP Templates**

9. **Train the Data Warehouse Users**

10. **Deploy the Data Warehouse**

11. **Begin Data Warehouse Support**

> **"We have met the enemy and he is us."**
> *Pogo (Walt Kelly)*

Step 1:   Practice the Due Diligence of Our Profession

Many tools, methods, and disciplines are available to assist with managing a software implementation or development process. However, our projects often fail because we choose not to use them. An article in the April 15, 2006, copy of *CIO* magazine by Allen Holmes illustrates this point well. The article is titled "Maine's Medicaid Mistakes." The byline follows: "Maine's attempt to build a Medicaid claims processing system is a classic example of how not to run a massive project." Following is how Holmes describes some of the problems:

> With 20/20 hindsight they can now look back and see where the project went wrong. Hiring developers that had no experience in developing Medicaid systems was the first mistake. And that was compounded by the decision to build a new and relatively unproven technology platform for the entire system rather than, as other states had done, integrating a web based portal with back-end legacy systems. Thirdly, IT switched over to the new system overnight with no backup system in case something was wrong. And making matters worse, no end-to-end testing or training was conducted before the switchover. Indeed, the story of the Maine Medicaid claims system is a classic example of how not to develop, deploy and manage an advanced web services system. (pp.46-54)

Holmes quotes Dick Thompson, then head of procurement for the state of Maine and now CIO: "By the first of March, it was clear that we were missing any sort of basic management of this project and were in complete defensive mode. We could not see our way out of this."

According to Holmes, "as of press time (for the article), Maine was the only state in the union not in compliance with the Health Insurance Portability and Accountability Act of 1996."

While most of our projects are not of this scope, many of our IT projects are very visible and have significant impact on the businesses we support. We have work tools and methodologies to keep ourselves out of trouble! My concern, after a 40-year hardware and software provisioning career, is that we, as a profession, are becoming complacent and lazy. We need to learn again how to use our work tools. Data warehouse development should be managed using, at the least, the following established IT work tools:

1. System Development Life Cycle methodology
2. Statement of Work
3. Request for Proposal
4. Project Management methodology

Using a System Development Life Cycle Methodology

A Traditional SDLC Process

The formal process by which organizations build computer-based systems is known as a System Development Life Cycle (SDLC). A traditional SDLC contains six phases that have a specific purpose and facilitate activities such as fact finding, documentation, presentation, estimation, measurement, feasibility analysis, project management, and process management. All these activities identify information necessary to develop a system that meets user needs.

The six phases are as follows:

1. *Preliminary Investigation*

   Management determines there is a problem with an existing information system or business process. A business or systems analyst does an initial study to determine preliminary costs, constraints, and benefits. He or she documents initial objectives, defines the nature and scope of the problem, and proposes alternative solutions. Finally, the analyst prepares, submits, and reviews a preliminary plan. Management determines the feasibility of moving to the next phase of the SDLC.

2. *Systems Analysis*

   A business or systems analyst performs an in-depth investigation of the problem and documents requirements for a new system. He or she gathers and analyzes the data, documents the process flows, prepares overview models, determines existing conditions and actions, and documents existing business rules. The analyst documents and presents the systems analysis phase results to management in three parts:

   a. An explanation of how the existing system works
   b. Problems with the existing system
   c. Requirements for a new system, including recommendations on what to do next

   Management reviews the in-depth analysis and determines the feasibility of moving to the next phase of the SDLC.

3. *Systems Design*

   An analyst creates detailed diagrams, charts, and models for a new system. He or she documents conditions and actions, documents business rules, and may create a prototype of the new system. The analyst prepares detailed design requirements for inputs, processing, outputs, storage, systems audits and controls, and backup/restore. Then, the analyst writes a report and presents it to management, who in turn decides whether or not to move to the next phase.

4. *Systems Development or Acquisition*

   A new system, both hardware and software, may be purchased. Programmers, monitored by analysts, may build a new system or enhance the old one. Testers test the system for quality. Management reviews system function and testing results for quality and decides whether or not to move to the next phase.

5. *Systems Implementation*

   Data, people, and processes are converted from the old system to the new system. Final documentation is prepared (technical and user). Users are trained. The new system is put into operation.

6. *Systems Maintenance*

   Periodic audits and evaluations of the system are completed. Analysts and programmers maintain, repair, and enhance the system until it is obsolete. Then the SDLC begins again for a new system.

Appendix B presents a diagram of the traditional SDLC process.

<u>Staged Delivery</u>

Another name for an SDLC is a staged delivery system. Software functionality is developed and delivered in stages. Four of the major benefits of staged delivery are as follows:

1. *Critical function is available earlier.*

   The stages of a staged delivery system are designed to deliver the software's most important function first.

2. *Risks are reduced early.*

   Staged delivery emphasizes planning and risk management throughout a project. Delivering a product in stages reduces the technical risk of unsuccessful integration because it forces integration to occur more often than it would if the product were delivered at the end of the project.

3. *Problems become evident earlier.*

   When releases are planned early and often, frequent progress reports are generated. Either the release is on time or it is not!

4. *Top management likes this approach because they begin to see an earlier return on the software investment.*

Staged delivery does have some notable costs. It increases project overhead because of the time needed to prepare the software for a releasable state multiple times, test and retest software, and perform version control tasks. Staged delivery is not a silver bullet. However, the additional overhead may be a small price to pay for improved status visibility, quality visibility, flexibility, estimate accuracy, and risk reduction.

NASA SEL Dos and Don'ts

The Software Engineering Lab (SEL) at NASA is one of the most successful software development organizations in the world. SEL has published a document that contains lessons learned from the last 20 years of software development. This document contains nine dos and eight don'ts. The first of the nine dos is to *create and follow a software development plan.* Appendix E contains a summary, prepared by Steve McConnell (1998), of the dos and don'ts from NASA's *Recommended Approach to Software Development.*

Extreme Programming (XP) – A New Paradigm

Ken Beck (2000) in *Extreme Programming Explained: Embrace Change* states that the basic software development problem is risk: "Software development fails to deliver value. This failure has huge economic and human impact. We need to find a new way to develop software" (Beck, 2000, p. 3). Beck proposes the need to control four variables in projects: cost, time, quality, and scope. He also states that all methodologies are based upon fear, and XP reflects his fear of the following:

- Doing work that doesn't matter
- Having projects canceled because not enough progress is made
- Making bad business decisions
- Having business people force bad technical decisions
- Coming to the end of a systems building career and concluding that he should have spent more time with the kids
- Doing work he is not proud of

Beck (2000) has written a set of development practices (the basics of XP) to help eliminate those fears. The following is an overview of XP practices:

1. *The planning game* – The scope of the next release should be quickly determined by combining business priorities and technical estimates. As reality overtakes the plan, update the plan.
2. *Small releases* – A simple version of the software should be put into production quickly, and then new versions released on a very short cycle.
3. *Metaphor* – All development should be guided with a simple shared story of how the system works.
4. *Simple design* – The system should be designed as simply as possible at any given moment. Extra complexity is removed as soon as it is discovered.
5. *Testing* – Programmers continually write unit tests that must run flawlessly for development to continue. Customers write tests, demonstrating that features are finished.
6. *Recapturing* – Programmers restructure the system, without changing its behavior, to remove duplication, improve communication, simplify, or add flexibility.

7. *Pair programming* – All production code is written with two programmers at one machine.

8. *Collective ownership* – Anyone can change any code anywhere in the system at any time.

9. *Continuous integration* – The system should be integrated and built many times a day, every time a task is completed.

10. *40-hour week* – As a rule, the work week should be no more than 40 hours. Never work overtime a second week in a row.

11. *On-site customer* – A real, live user should be included on the team, available full-time to answer questions.

12. *Coding standards* – Programmers write all code in accordance with rules, emphasizing communication through the code.

Each of these SDLC practices requires that a standard development methodology be defined and used!

When software developers are undisciplined, working outside a defined and measurable methodology, managers are placed in the indefensible position of not being able to explain project time overruns, functional deficiencies, or out-of-control costs. Managers must study, understand, and establish system development methodologies, such as those described above, or develop and implement their own. There is, of course, another option. According to Beck, the alternative option involves standing in long lines and filling out many forms!

Using a Statement of Work

Data gathered in traditional SDLC phases 1, 2, and 3 are used to create a Statement of Work (SOW). A SOW is a narrative description of the products, the services, or the results to be supplied by a vendor. Dr. Harold Kerzner reminds us that project planning cannot be accomplished unless all of the necessary information becomes available at project initiation (*Project Management*, Seventh Edition, p. 564). The information requirements are as follows:

- Statement of Work (SOW)
- Project specifications
- Milestone schedule
- Work breakdown structure (WBS)

Statement of Work (SOW)

The purpose of a SOW is to do the following:
- Define the scope of a project.
- Define the participants and their responsibilities.
- Force both agreements and disagreements of the project scope to surface early.
- Serve as a formal contract between a project manager, project sponsor and the customer.

The sections of a SOW are as follows:
- *Introduction.* Provides a brief description of the project.
- *Goals and Objectives.* Documents project goals and objectives. Defines deliverables, measures of success, and doneness.
- *Scope.* Defines project boundaries and functions to be included and excluded.
- *Planning Assumptions.* Defines critical assumptions made by the project manager.
- *Stakeholders.* Identifies and defines key stakeholders. Stakeholders are individuals or groups whose interests need to be considered during the project.
- *Project Resources.* Identifies key resources involved in the project along with responsibilities for each of the resources.
- *Milestones.* Includes a schedule of project milestones.
- *Budget.* Includes the project budget by milestone.

- *Amendments.* Identifies the steps all parties agree to follow when any change to the project or SOW is required.
- *Signatures.* Records the dated signatures of the customer, project manager, and project sponsor, signifying agreement to all items presented in the SOW.

Appendix K contains a sample SOW template.

Lesson Learned

- Do not agree to a fixed-price, fixed-term contract for a project without thoroughly defining the project scope.

Project Specifications

According to PMBOK®, project specifications are "a *document* that specifies, in a complete, precise, verifiable manner, the *requirements*, *design, behavior*, or other characteristics of a *system, component, product*, *result* or *service* and, often, the *procedures* for determining whether these provisions have been satisfied." Project specifications provide the standard for pricing a proposal.

Milestone Schedule

A milestone schedule lists significant events in the project schedule, such as tasks constraining future work or marking the completion of a major deliverable.

Work Breakdown Structure

A work breakdown structure (WBS) is the hierarchy of tasks in a project and can have multiple levels. Each WBS level depicts the project at a different level of detail. Creating a work breakdown structure is the process used for subdividing major project deliverables and project work into smaller, more manageable components. In project management vernacular, this process is called decomposition.

Using a Request for Proposal

A Request for Proposal (RFP) is a detailed list of questions submitted to vendors of software or other services to determine how well their products can meet the organization's specific requirements. An RFP is used to convey understanding of a particular business situation to the stakeholders and vendors who would be involved in providing products or services to support that business situation.

An RFP should contain, at a minimum, the following:
- Cover or invitation to bid letter
- Technology overview describing the technology environment of your company
- Discussion of all the aspects of the current business requirement
- Set of vendor response requirements
- Description of vendor response evaluation criteria

Developing an RFP Format

In the February 21, 2003, issue of DM direct newsletter, Randy Law provided guidelines for creating an effective RFP for business intelligence and data warehouse projects. Law identified an eight-point outline to serve as a high-level table of contents:

1. *Administrative information:* Tell suppliers where and when to submit the proposal, provide a list of important dates, define communication between client and supplier, provide the format and content requirements for preparing the proposal, provide proposal evaluation criteria, and provide RHP contact names and addresses.

2. *Project overview and scope:* Give suppliers a summary statement of your business problem, goals and objectives. Clearly state the current sources of pain that, if relieved, will provide the greatest value to your organization.

3.   *Solution requirements:* Be as specific as possible about the following requirements for the delivered solution: standard reports and queries, data subject areas/elements/metrics, security, meta data, system automation, data quality and cleansing, end users, performance specifications and constraints (for example, hardware, software, network). Provide the supplier with an overview of the existing source and reporting systems and the approach or philosophy (e.g., Inmon, Kimball, etc.) preferences that you may have. Focus on defining your high-value reporting requirements and describe the nature of your existing source systems from which to feed your reports.

4.   *Management requirements:* State the need for a development methodology, project management, staffing, site preparation responsibilities, delivery schedule and plan, systems operations and maintenance, training, and documentation requirements.

5.   *Supplier qualifications:* Request a brief history of the suppliers' firm, financial health, development and maintenance offerings, relationship with other suppliers, evidence of technical skills, staff and resources, references, and location of consultants.

6.   *Pricing:* Request a pricing break out by hardware, software, consulting services, maintenance, training, documentation, ongoing license fees, travel, and expenses.

7.   *Contracts and agreements:* Request a sample master agreement/contract, maintenance contracts, warranty, hardware license agreements, nondisclosure agreements, and relevant government regulations. Provide a sample master

agreement/contract to the supplier if you already have a good one –
it can spot issues early and speed the process considerably.

8.   *Appendices:* Provide the supplier with sample user reports, detailed
information regarding your source systems, list of existing
equipment/software, standards used within the company, and
tentative project plans with dates, if appropriate.

The value of providing all this information is that the guesswork is taken out
of what products and services are being requested, the nature of your
existing environment, the form and content of the requested proposal, who
is responsible for what, and how you and prospective suppliers will
coordinate communications. An RFP document containing the above
information puts you in the position of making well-informed decisions
regarding which supplier can best serve your needs after receiving your
supplier proposals in response to your RFP. Ultimately, it lowers your risk.

Dr. Kimball states that the RPF process is often over-engineered. The caution,
then, is to provide RFP *substance* and eliminate sizzle!

Appendix C contains a sample RFP outline from the CD accompanying the *Data
Warehouse Management Handbook* (Kachur, 2000).

Using a Project Management Methodology

The graphic below represents my approach to understanding and applying project management.

Read This	Then This	Do This!

Figure 1.1

- *Project Management – A Systems Approach to Planning, Scheduling, Controlling*, written by Dr. Harold Kerzner, is the academic classic project management publication.

- *A Guide to the Project Management Body of Knowledge (PMBOK®)*, published by the Project Management Institute, is the ANSI standard and the primary industry resource for project management practitioners desiring certification as project managers.

- *Project Management Methodology – A Practical Guide for the Next Millennium*," by Ralph L. Kliem, Irwin S Ludin, and Ken L. Robertson, presents a straightforward and easy to apply methodology (P^2M^2) for bringing management oversight to a project.

P²M² Methodology Overview

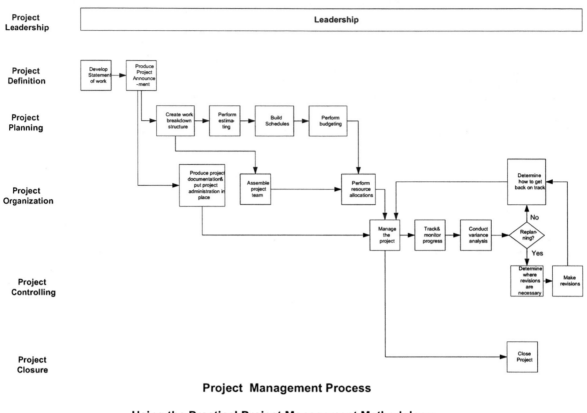

Project Management Process

Using the Practical Project Management Methodology

(P²M²)

Figure 1.2

1. *Leading*

   Effective project management requires strong leadership. Leadership is multifaceted, comprising a wide range of various activities. The first is motivation. Project managers must motivate everyone on a project, not just team members; they serve as a catalyst for getting people to participate effectively. They also must act as a catalyst to get the customer, the project team, and management to work together harmoniously to meet project goals and objectives. Project managers set an example by establishing performance standards to follow and expect others to do likewise.

2. *Defining*

   It is essential that major goals and objectives of a project be defined. Project definition involves identifying at a high level the who, what, when, where, why, and how of a project. Specific objectives to be reached must be defined. The objectives must be measurable and will serve as benchmarks to determine how well the project progresses.

3. *Planning*

   The project manager and the project team will determine, to the best of their abilities, a series of actions to complete the project. To accomplish this major feat, the project manager must initiate a planning process. He or she will determine the tasks required to reach the goals and objectives documented in the definition component. Task listings will be used to create valid schedules. The project manager and the project team will also determine which tasks are significant and which are not. Effective planning requires identifying the most critical tasks to complete. During planning, project managers also will identify the required resources. After the resources have been identified, project managers will determine how much money to spend on each task and on the entire project. Obstacles will be identified, such as lack of time. Areas where cooperation is lacking will also be identified.

4. *Organization*

   The project manager then will establish a structure to maximize the efficiency and effectiveness of the project. A communications structure for the project will be developed. Communications must be both vertical and horizontal, and project managers will hold the right meetings at the right time with the right people.

5. *Controlling*

   The project manager will ensure that the project proceeds according to plans that maximize the effectiveness of the organizational structure. Controlling involves receiving feedback on the project status, and if necessary, taking whatever action is needed to regain control. Maintaining effective control involves receiving affirmation in three areas: schedule, budget, and quality.

   The project manager will perform tracking and monitoring to assess whether or not progress is being made. Tracking involves collecting information about what has been done on a project to determine its progress. Monitoring entails looking not only at the past, but also the future. The project manager will use this information to predict whether or not the project is on schedule.

   The project manager will also track and monitor costs, accounting for every dollar spent and ascertaining how much money will be needed to complete the project.

   The project manager will also track and monitor the quality of the output from the project. To track and monitor quality, project managers must install measures to ensure that quality of the project teams output is maintained.

   The project manager will also determine variants regarding schedule, cost, and quality. Periodically, the project manager may have to re-plan. Re-planning should occur sparingly. Too much re-planning indicates that the project manager has little control over the project and may be construed as conveniently rubber-stamping the current circumstances.

6. *Closing*

Closing the project will not be treated nonchalantly. The project manager will compile data and convert it into information to assess performance and provide lessons learned for future projects. He will document the experience and wisdom to enable future project managers to learn from their experiences, both the negative and positive, such as best practices. The project manager will also smooth the transition from a project environment to an operational one.

Appendix D. presents a further review of P^2M^2 developed from the Kliem, Ludin, and Robertson (1997) materials and was used for training my staff.

Appendix H contains Dr. Harold Kerzner's sixteen points to project management maturity. Point number one is "Adopt a project management methodology and use it consistently."

If our projects fail because we do not take advantage of proven tools, like the ones discussed above, then we have no one to blame but ourselves for the failure. And when our projects fail because of our lack of discipline, then the sad truth is that, in the eyes of technology users, our profession has failed.

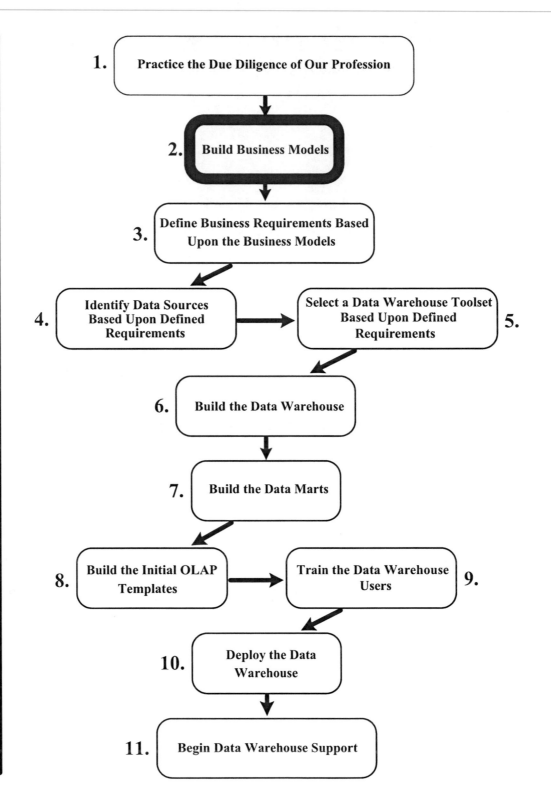

<< Data Warehouse Implementation Methodology Steps >>

1. Practice the Due Diligence of Our Profession

2. Build Business Models

3. Define Business Requirements Based Upon the Business Models

4. Identify Data Sources Based Upon Defined Requirements

5. Select a Data Warehouse Toolset Based Upon Defined Requirements

6. Build the Data Warehouse

7. Build the Data Marts

8. Build the Initial OLAP Templates

9. Train the Data Warehouse Users

10. Deploy the Data Warehouse

11. Begin Data Warehouse Support

> "Competence goes beyond words.
> It is a leader's ability to say it, plan it, and do it in such a way
> that others know that you know how,
> and know that they want to follow you."
> *John C. Maxwell*

Step 2:   Build Business Models

Once (and not until) we identify and understand the due diligence work tools that will be used to provide management and control of our data warehouse project, we can start documenting business structure, operation, process, and function. We will do this at a high level first, using modeling. The modeling process facilitates developing project consensus at all levels – from the board room to the back room. Many areas of business operation will probably need to be demystified. Unfortunately, too many business processes are the result of years of tacit knowledge instead of proactive planning to make them effective and efficient. Are we doing the right thing? Are we doing it the best possible way? Answering those two questions will very often lead to process re-engineering that will greatly improve the business. The information captured and documented in this step will be used in step 3 to define requirements.

Corporate Technology Overlay Model - The Place to Start

Presenting a high-level view of how technologies are overlaid across an organization prior to building the necessary technology infrastructure is helpful. The following model depicts six interdependent domains that are merged to apply computer technology across an organization.

Following are the domains:

> Software Domain
>
> Hardware Domain
>
> Data Transport Domain
>
> Telecommunications Domain
>
> Service and Support Domain
>
> Technology Management and Leadership Domain

The model lists specific disciplines and levels of understanding needed within each of the interdependent domains.

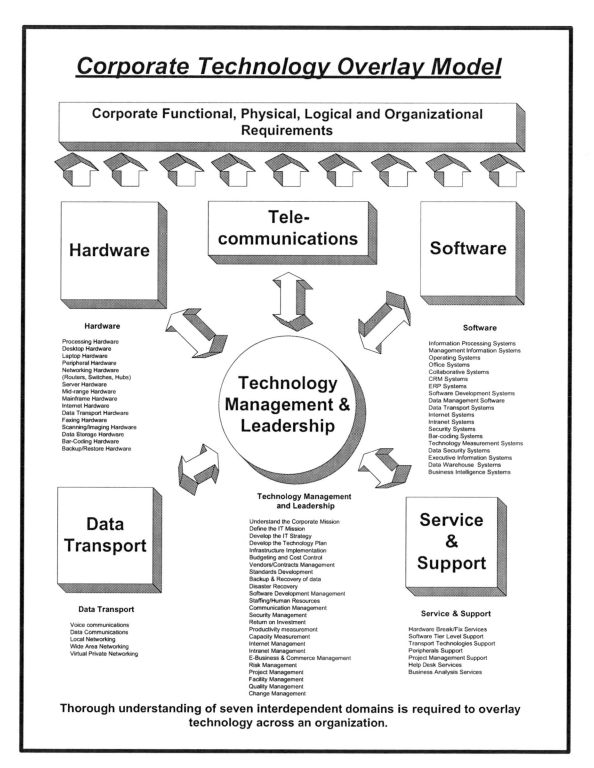

Figure 2.1

Building a technology infrastructure without first defining the corporate mission, preparing a strategic plan, designing a corporate business architecture, and developing a technology plan may lead to a misaligned infrastructure allowing many users to have access to unneeded technology services. Building an infrastructure requires understanding of the organization's business model. That understanding drives the requirements of the other domains.

The Software Domain

Software is the term used to describe the instructions that tell the hardware how to perform a task. Hardware is useless without software, and software is the user's primary tool! Once the business model is understood, business functions that will be automated must be determined. Business functions are automated using information processing systems. Information processing systems are generally categorized by type:

- *Operating System Software*
  "Operating system software coordinates the various parts of the computer system and mediates between application software and computer hardware" (Laudon & Laudon, 2002, p. 173).

  Application software needed to run a business drives selection of the operating system hardware and software. For example, specialized software needed to support the business may only run on an IBM System i.

- *Transaction Processing Software*
  Transaction processing systems are the basic business systems that serve the operational level of an organization. These systems perform routine daily tasks and record the routine daily transactions necessary to conduct business. Examples of transaction processing systems are human resources, payroll, accounts payable, accounts receivable, general ledger, sales order entry,

billing, inventory control, shipping, and many more. Transaction processing systems record daily business transactions, sort, list, and update the systems, and generate detailed reports. Users are primarily operational level staff.

- *Office Software*

  Office systems are designed to increase the level of productivity across all levels of an organization. Typical office systems are word processing systems, spread sheet preparation systems, e-mail systems, collaborative systems, faxing systems, imaging systems, scheduling systems, voice mail systems, and video conferencing systems, to name a few. Certain office software systems, such as scientific or engineering software, used by members of recognized professions, are called knowledge work systems. These systems are typically used for modeling, simulation, and business discipline compliance such as Department of Transportation regulation assessment.

- *Management Information Software*

  Management Information Software is typically used to provide middle management with online summary and exception reporting of high volume transactions for an organization's basic operations. These systems typically provide summary information in such areas as sales management, inventory control, and budgeting.

- *Decision Support Software*

  Decision support systems provide information at the organization's management level that combines transaction or summary data and analytical models to support non-routine decision-making. These systems often bring in information from outside the organization such as competitive pricing and market share. These systems are used to do analysis such as developing customer profiles, determining customer buying patterns, and determining new store locations.

- *Executive Support Software*

  These systems support the organization's strategic management level and typically address non-routine decision-making through advanced graphics. An ESS would be used to help develop the organization's strategic plan. These systems pool data from diverse internal and external sources and make information available in easy-to-use forms. ESS systems are used to quickly identify problems that are threats to the strategic direction.

The Hardware Domain

Software selection drives hardware selection. Software services being provided to the organization must be understood prior to selection of a hardware environment. As stated earlier, certain software may require specific processing or input/output hardware. My facetious hardware (as compared to software) definition is this: If you can kick it, it's hardware! The hardware overlay can be divided into three general domains:

- *Processing Hardware*

  A computer-processing platform must be selected. Processing hardware platforms are generally classified as mainframe, mid-range, or server-based with server-based processors being the least expensive and mainframe processors the most expensive. The processor, sometimes called the system unit or system cabinet, contains the circuitry that actually executes the operating software instructions.

- *Input/Output Hardware*

  Input/output hardware performs the actual interface between computer users and the processing hardware. Input hardware devices translate data into a form the processor can use. Output hardware devices translate information processed by the computer into a form that humans can understand.

Computer software needed by an organization's employees to perform tasks is what drives the selection of input and output hardware. Input hardware devices are equipment such as keyboards, microphones, mice, scanners, digital cameras, tape drives, CD readers, and light pens. Output hardware devices include equipment such as printers, monitors, speakers, writeable CD's, and tape drives. Some devices perform both input and output functions.

- *Storage Hardware*

  Equipment that electronically stores data or programs permanently on disk or tape is called secondary storage. These devices can be thought of as an electronic filing cabinet. Data are stored electronically until needed. In most cases, only a copy of the data is retrieved from the electronic filing cabinet; however, when necessary, the updated information may replace an original file or document.

The Data Transport Domain

The data transport overlay is essentially an electronic highway to which shared processors, input/output devices, and telephone systems are connected in order to exchange information (called packets) using either analog or digital technology.

A manager *must* have a working level of knowledge regarding transport technologies.

Telecommunications Domain

Connection of shared devices is called networking. Networks can use both internal and external circuits to transport analog or digital signal. External transport of signal very often uses circuits provided by telephone companies. The network model in Figure 2.5 shows an overview of the data transport overlay in place at Rumpke Consolidated Companies. Two types of data packets, analog and digital, can be transmitted electronically via telecommunications.

- *Analog Signals*

  Analog signals travel across telephone cables as electromagnetic waves. Analog travel is expressed in frequency. Frequency refers to the number of times per second that a wave oscillates in a complete cycle from its starting point to its end point. Frequency is measured in hertz (Hz). For example, an electromagnetic wave that oscillates back and forth 10 times per second has a speed of 10Hz. Analog services, such as voice, radio, and TV signals, oscillate within a specified range of frequencies. Frequencies that analog services use are expressed in abbreviated forms:

  - Kilohertz (kHz) = thousands of cycles per second
    Voice is carried in the frequency range of .3 kHz to 3.3 kHz.
  - Megahertz (MHz) = millions of cycles per second
    Analog cable TV signals are carried in the frequency range of 54 MHz to 750 MHz.
  - Gigahertz (GHz) = billions of cycles per second
    Most analog microwave towers operate at between 2 and 12 GHz.

  Analog signals have two major impairments:
  - As an analog signal is transmitted, it loses strength due to resistance and must be amplified.

♦ Amplified signals often contain noise, which causes static. Static causes errors in the transmission.

- *Digital Signals*

Digital signals have a number of advantages over analog signals - higher speeds, clearer voice quality, fewer errors, and less complex equipment requirements. Instead of waves, digital signals are transmitted in the form of binary bits. The term binary refers to the fact that there are only two values for transmitted voice and data bits – on or off. Digital signals also decrease in volume over distance, fade, and are subject to interference (static). Digital signals can be repaired more easily than analog signals. Digital signals are also faster than analog signals, measured in terabits (trillions of cycles per second). A terabit is equal to 1,000 gigabits.

- *LANs, MANs, and WANs*

The difference between LANs, MANs, and WANs is the distance over which devices can communicate with others.

- *Bandwidth – Measuring Capacity*

In telecommunications, bandwidth refers to capacity and is expressed differently in analog and digital transmissions. Analog bandwidth is measured in megahertz (MHz), while digital bandwidth is measured in bits per second. For example, a T-1 line has a bandwidth of 1.54 Mbps (megabits per second).

- *Protocols*

Protocols allow devices to communicate with each other. They provide a common language and set of transmission rules. For example, devices communicating over the Internet use a suite of protocols called TCP/IP.

- *Architectures*

  Architectures tie dissimilar protocols together. For instance, IBM developed the architecture called SNA to enable its devices to talk together. The International Standards Organization (ISO) developed a protocol called Open System Interconnection (OSI) to allow devices from multiple vendors to communicate with each other. Both LANs and the Internet are based upon concepts developed by the OSI for a layered, open architecture.

- *The Public Switched Network*

  In the United States, voice and data signals travel over the public switched network. This network has two basic services – switched and dedicated. The main difference between switched and dedicated services is that switched services are dialable and dedicated services are not. With switched services, the connections made by dialing a phone number are flexible, based upon the phone number dialed. With dedicated services, the links between locations are permanent.

- *Specialized Digital Network Services*

  The following table presents eight specialized digital network services, places they are typically used, and how they are used.

Network Service	Places typically used	How typically used
T-1 24 voice or data channels	Medium to large organizations	Access to Internet and long distance companies' backbones (the high traffic portion of networks)
T-3 672 voice or data channels	Large organization, Internet service providers	Access to long distance companies, ISP connections to the Internet, high-speed connections between company sites
BRI ISDN Two voice or data channels plus one signaling channel	High-end residential customers	Video conferencing, telecommuting, Internet access
PRI ISDN 23 voice or data channels plus one signaling channel	Internet service providers, PBX's, automatic call distributors (ACD's)	Call centers, room size video conferencing, remote access to corporate databases
DSL (Digital Subscriber Lines) 128 KBPS to 6 megabits	Telecommuters, corporations, ISP's, high-end residential customers	Remote access to corporate databases and internet access; some types used for voice
Frame Relay 56 KBPS to 45 megabit access to value-added networks	Medium to large commercial customers	Public, primary data network service for LAN to LAN connections and remote access
ATM (Asynchronous Transfer Mode) 56 KPBS to 2.5 gigabits	Telcos, ISP's, frame relay networks, and large organizations (e.g., universities)	Used to switch high-usage backbone voice, video and data traffic
SONET (Synchronous Optical Network) Up to 129,000 channels on fiber optic cable	Telephone companies	Multiplexes traffic from multiple customers onto fiber optic cables; provides extra reliability in the local loop and in carrier networks

Specialized Digital Network Services (Dodd, 1999, p. 180)

Figure 2.2

- *Network Data Transport*

  Much of the media employed in conventional telecommunications technology can also be employed in the construction of local area networks. Three transport media (cabling systems) are most often used: twisted-pair wires, coaxial cable, and fiber optic links. A major factor in choosing a particular local area network is the type of physical cabling that the LAN uses. In a very simple case, a LAN may be used to link a number of computers and other intelligent devices that are in the physical proximity. In this case, the type of wiring may be of little concern. In more advanced applications, such as connecting devices throughout an entire building, the type of cabling the LAN employs may be the most important characteristic of the network.

Service and Support Domain

The information technology department provides service and support for hardware, software, and data transport technology. Service and support may also come from sources outside the organization. In addition, support services such as project management, business analysis, and help desk services may be provided to support the organization. Some services may be required 24 hours per day, 365 days a year, depending upon the corporate business model.

The Technology Management and Leadership Domain

An argument could be made that technology management requirements would be virtually the same regardless of the business model. An argument could also be made that many management requirements could be different. There is, however, *no argument* that technology management has direct responsibility for all aspects of computer technology within an organization. That responsibility includes assisting in strategy definition, technology architecture definition, technology planning, technology implementation, and daily operational management. The Technology Overlay Model in Figure 2.1 lists many of technology management's responsibilities. Missing from the list shown in the model is *"Whatever it takes to provide reliable computer technology to the organization."*

If managers assume the responsibility for technology that must be available to meet business goals, they must also accept the understanding that technology application to business is now a lifelong learning profession. In order to exploit technology effectively to create a competitive advantage for an employer, technology providers must do the following:

- Continue to learn everything about technology that they can!
- Continue to learn everything about business that they can!
- Continue to learn everything about their employer's business that they can!

And finally, they must accept a 24/7/365 availability commitment to their employer.

They must do whatever it takes!

The Corporate Technology Overlay Model provides a high level view of domains required to facilitate building an infrastructure. Now, the actual infrastructure planning and implementation model must be defined.

Infrastructure and Alignment Planning Model

The following is an Infrastructure Planning and Alignment model. The model organizes issues that must be defined to understand technology requirements from mission statement to infrastructure deployment. The model is based on the following understanding:

- *Correct strategy* cannot be developed without defining the corporate mission.

- *Correct technology architecture* and the resulting technology plan cannot be developed without a corporate-level strategic plan.
- *Correct infrastructure* is dependent upon the corporate mission definition, strategic planning, and development of a technology plan to support the articulated mission and strategy.
- *Infrastructure definition* includes all shared and non-shared hardware, software, data transport, support services, processes, and management understanding required to meet the specifications of the technology plan.

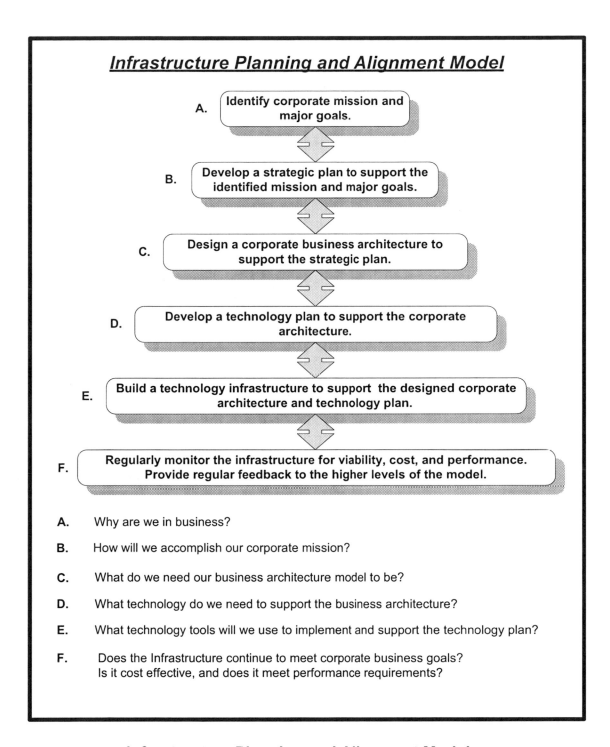

Infrastructure Planning and Alignment Model

Figure 2.3

A. *Identify the corporate mission and major goals.*

Why are we in business?

The corporate mission statement drives every corporate activity. It identifies why a company is in business. For example, the RCC mission statement is to "maximize the growth of Rumpke in market size, market share, and profitability by providing outstanding services to our customers and employees while maintaining regulatory compliance."

A company's stakeholders develop the mission statement. Stakeholders are those individuals or groups that have an interest or stake in the company, in both what the company does and how well the company performs. The major goals of the organization are also defined at this level. The mission statement and corporate goals should announce strategic intent. Examples of strategic intent would be verbiage such as these: "be number one" or "deliver exceptional products or services." Without a stated mission and articulated goals, a strategic plan cannot be developed, and this plan is the next step toward infrastructure planning. Remember again the famous quote attributed to Yogi Berra: *"If you don't know where you're going, you may end up somewhere else!"*

B. *Develop a strategic plan to support the mission and major goals.*

How will we accomplish our corporate mission?

Developing a strategic plan requires asking (and answering!) many questions. For example:

- What businesses are we in?
- What is our *core* business?
- What are our strengths, weaknesses, opportunities, and threats (S.W.O.T. analysis)?

- How will we approach the sales and marketing of our services?
- What are our KPIs (Key Performance Indicators)?
- What are our CSFs (Critical Success Factors)?

  Figure 3.1 contains an example of RCC KPIs and CSFs.

- What will our business model be? Global? Centralized? Decentralized?
- Will accounting and other back office services be centralized or distributed?
- Do we need e-commerce to be successful?
- Do we need e-business to be successful?

Such questions, and many more, require answers before a strategic plan can be developed, and they must be answered before a business architecture and technology plan can be prepared.

C. Design a corporate business architecture to support the strategic plan.

What do we need our business architecture model to be?

After the strategic plan has been developed, business architecture will be developed to support the strategic plan. Again, we will be required to ask and answer many questions. Answers to these questions will be organized for preparation of a technology plan. Issues addressed in the strategic plan will drive the business architecture questions. For example:

- How simple or complicated do we want our business model to be?
- Should we lease or purchase equipment?
- How much growth should we prepare for?
- Should we use consultants or develop in-house capabilities for technology?
- How dependent upon technology do we want to be?
- What business functions need to be automated?
- How much money are we willing to spend on technology?
- What is the functional business model?
- What is the geographic business model?

- What is the logical business model?
- What corporate services will be centralized?
- What corporate services will be distributed?
- How do we want to communicate with each other?
- How do we want to communicate with our customers?
- What are the measures for success?

The answers to these questions will drive the preparation of a technology plan.

D. Develop a technology plan to support the corporate architecture.

What technology do we need to support the business architecture?

The technology plan will address the use of many interdependent technologies and services that will be an overlay across the defined architecture. Domains described in the Corporate Technology Overlay Model can be used to segment technology and services needing consideration to support the architecture:

- Software
- Hardware
- Data Transport
- Telecommunications
- Service and Support
- Technology Management and Leadership

Information technology managers must have, or have access to, thorough understanding of each technology domain. The technology plan must describe how each technology domain can be exploited to meet the requirements of the corporate architecture.

E. Build a technology infrastructure to support the corporate architecture and technology plan.

What technology tools will we use to implement and support the technology plan?

Once requirements for all domains of the Corporate Technology Overlay Model have been identified and documented, building the infrastructure can begin. The infrastructure building process requires written plans and a business case that must be approved by senior management, enabling monies to be procured. A project plan must also be drafted – see the SDLC and Project Management Methodology (P^2M^2) in Figure 1.2 – answering the who, what, where, when, why, and how questions for each domain. P^2M^2 contains a generic project plan for organizing the building process of the hardware and data transport infrastructure. Building the infrastructure will be organized around the domains shown in the Corporate Technology Overlay Model. Begin with the software questions. When corporate architecture is defined, certain questions will be raised – what software will be needed to deliver the services required to answer those questions? Start with the software list defined in the Corporate Technology Overlay Model.

- Information processing systems
- Management information systems
- Operation systems
- Office systems
- Collaborative systems
- CRM systems
- ERP systems
- Software development systems
- Data management software
- Data transport systems

- Internet systems
- Intranet systems
- Security systems
- Bar-coding systems
- Technology measurement systems
- Data security systems
- Executive information systems
- Data warehouse systems
- Business intelligence systems

Then, add any additional systems that are needed for the organization.

Once the software has been defined (remember that application software selection drives the operating software selection, which in turn drives hardware platform selection), begin defining hardware requirements. Again, start with the list shown in the Corporate Technology Overlay Model.

- Processing hardware
- Desktop hardware
- Laptop hardware
- Peripheral hardware
- Networking hardware (routers, switches, hubs)
- Server hardware
- Mid-range hardware
- Mainframe hardware
- Internet Hardware
- Data transport hardware
- Faxing hardware
- Scanning/Imaging hardware
- Data storage hardware

- Bar-coding hardware
- Backup/restore hardware

Then, as with software, add any additional hardware needed for the organization (e.g., tablets, GPS equipment, automated scales, bar coding).

The data transport domain must be considered as software and hardware are being defined.

- How will we deliver voice, video, and data signal? Within the organization? Outside the organization?
- What bandwidth will be needed?
- What redundancy will be needed?
- Will we need Virtual Private Networking (VPN) capability?
- Will we need RAS (Remote Access Services) capability?
- What packet transport protocol best suits our needs?

Communications technologies are very specialized and complicated. Unless you have, or have access to, this expertise, get help!

Finally, the service and support requirements for the infrastructure must be defined. Again, start with the list on the Corporate Technology Overlay Model:

- Hardware break/fix services
- Software tier-level support
- Transport technologies support
- Peripherals support
- Project management support
- Help desk services
- Business analysis services

Add any additional specialized service and support capability needed to insure viability of the infrastructure.

F. Monitor the technology infrastructure.

Does the infrastructure continue to meet corporate business goals? Is it cost effective, and does it meet performance requirements?

Once the infrastructure is in place, management must establish key performance indicators (KPIs) and critical success factors (CSFs). Infrastructure must be monitored for viability, operating cost, and performance. Following are typical infrastructure monitoring metrics:

- Percent of customers satisfied with system availability
- Percent of customers satisfied with system response time
- Percent of customers satisfied with available software function
- Percent of customers satisfied with system simplicity of use
- Percent of customers satisfied with IT maintenance and support
- Percent of projects on time and under budget
- Percent of system capacity used as related to system capacity available
- IT budget as a percent of total budget

Technology managers must develop a measurement and reporting system to monitor how well the infrastructure (as well as the IT department!) is performing. A number of methodologies, such as the balanced scorecard, are applicable to monitoring and assessing Information technology.

Management Issues Encompassing Infrastructure

Technology management issues are many and varied. Review the topics listed on the Corporate Technology Overlay Model:

- Understanding the corporate mission
- Defining the information technology mission
- Developing the information technology strategy
- Developing a technology plan
- Designing and implementing infrastructure
- Budgeting and cost control
- Vendor contract management
- Standards development
- Information backup and recovery
- Disaster recovery
- Software development management
- Staffing and human resources
- Upward and downward management communications
- Security management
- Return on investment
- Productivity measurement
- Capacity measurement
- Internet management
- Intranet management
- E-business management
- E-commerce management
- Risk management
- Project management
- Facilities management
- Quality management

- Change management

Each technology manager must add and define any additional issues relevant to the infrastructure for which they have responsibility.

Strategies and tactics for each listed item must be developed, practiced, and changed when necessary. As stated earlier, technology management is now a lifelong learning profession and should not be approached any other way. Every statement made, every decision made, and every question asked in corporate information technology life must be done so with the full awareness of each domain represented in the Corporate Technology Overlay Model and each level in the Infrastructure Planning and Alignment Model. Technology managers must continually ask these questions: Does our approach support the corporate mission, strategy, architecture, and technology plan? If not, then why are we doing it?

Strategic Alignment

The critical component of strategically aligning business and technology is obvious. The organization must have a strategic plan. According to Brown and Topi (2000):

> The starting point for designing and implementing an effective infrastructure is the corporate strategy....A corporate strategy that articulates key processes is absolutely essential for designing an IT infrastructure because otherwise neither IT nor business management can define priorities. The vision peels back corporate complexities so that the infrastructure is built around simple, core processes. This peeling provides a solid foundation that can adapt to the dynamics of the business environment. Some firms have attempted to compensate for lack of clarity and corporate goals by spending more money on their infrastructures. Rather than determine what

kinds of communications they most need to enable, they invest in state-of-the-art technologies that should allow them to communicate with anyone, anytime, anywhere. Rather than determining what data standards are most crucial for meeting immediate customer needs, they attempt to design all-encompassing data models. This approach to infrastructure building is expensive and generally not fruitful. **Money is not a good substitute for planning.**

For organizations that do not have a basic strategic planning model, there are five steps to complete:

1. *Determine the corporate mission and major corporate goals.*
   A mission statement documents why the organization exists and what it should be doing. Major goals identify what the organization hopes to accomplish in near, medium, and long terms.
2. *Analyze the organization's external competitive environment to determine threats and opportunities.*
   This analysis identifies the competitive structure of the organization's industry group, its major rivals, and the development maturity of the industry.
3. *Analyze the organization's internal operating environment to identify weaknesses and strengths.*
   This analysis pinpoints weaknesses as well as strengths within the organization. One goal is to identify competitive advantage.
4. *Select strategies that correct the organization's weaknesses and build on the organization's strengths.*
   Hill and Jones (2001) identify four levels of strategy that need to be developed:

   - *Business-level strategy*
     The business-level strategy of a company encompasses the overall competitive theme that a company chooses to stress, the way it positions itself in the marketplace to gain competitive advantage, and

the different positioning strategies that can be used in different industry settings.

- *Functional-level strategy*

  Functional-level strategies are directed at improving the effectiveness of operations within a company, such as manufacturing, marketing, materials management, product development, and customer service.

- *Global strategy*

  Global strategies allow a company to expand its operations outside its home country.

- *Corporate-level strategy*

  Corporate-level strategy allows a company to determine what business it should be in to maximize the long-run profitability of the organization.

5. *Implement the strategy.*

   Hill and Jones (2001, p. 10) segment strategy implementation into four components:

   - Designing appropriate organizational structures
   - Designing control systems
   - Matching strategy, structure, and controls
   - Managing conflict, politics, and change

Identifying a company's strengths, weaknesses, opportunities, and threats is referred to as S.W.O.T. analysis. The primary purpose of S.W.O.T. analysis is to identify strategies that align a company's resources to the demands of the environment in which the company operates. S.W.O.T. analysis is designed to generate alternatives that build on the company's strengths, exploit opportunities, counter the threats, and correct company weaknesses.

Strategic planning is an ongoing process. A feedback loop is required. Once the strategy has been defined, it must be implemented. Once the strategy has been implemented, it must be monitored. Results from monitoring must be passed back to the corporate level to be used as input into the next round of strategic planning.

Steps to Creating a Strategic Plan – Another View

Sobel (1993, pp. 195-196) suggests three steps to corporate strategic planning, with each step containing a series of questions or statements:

- *Establish corporate objectives*
    1. What is the present condition of the market and our share of it?
    2. Who is the competition and to what extent do they pose a risk?
    3. What are our company's strengths and weaknesses?
    4. What will our future position be without change?
    5. Is this satisfactory?
    6. If our future position without change is not satisfactory, what can we do internally to improve things?
    7. If our future position without change is not satisfactory, what can we do externally to improve things?
    8. What will our future position be if we make these changes?
    9. Compare question 4 with question 8.
    10. Decide to maintain the status quo or make changes.

- *Create the plan*
    1. Analyze the nature of the business.
    2. Analyze the macro environment.
    3. Identify obstacles.
    4. Identify opportunities.
    5. Determine and qualify goals.
    6. Develop plans of action.
    7. Determine allocation of finances and other resources.
    8. Select methods to measure, review, and control procedures.

9. Submit the proposed written plan for review and approval.

- *Evaluate the plan*
    1. Does performance history provide adequate background, or do we need more information?
    2. Has the macro environment been adequately appraised?
    3. Have the capabilities of the organization been thoroughly examined?
    4. Have the best opportunities been identified?
    5. Have all opportunities and downside risks been identified?
    6. Have all possible alternative strategies been considered?
    7. Does the marketing mix flow logically from the chosen strategy?
    8. Are recommended projects necessary and properly funded?
    9. Are financial data clear and consistent?
    10. Have benchmarks in controls been established?
    11. Is the strategic plan compatible with prevailing attitudes, interests, and opinions (i.e., corporate culture, public image)?
    12. Is the strategic plan defensible?

Without strategic planning, regardless of the planning model used, information technology management will have difficulty developing a defensible infrastructure. Management may very well be substituting money for planning!

Putting the Strategic Plan into Action

Once a company has chosen a strategy to achieve its goals, that strategy must be put into action. Hill and Jones (2001, p. 10) break that action down into four main components:

- *Designing organizational structure*
    This component requires the allocation of roles and responsibilities for different aspects of the strategy to different managers and some units within the company.

- *Designing control systems*

  This component requires an organization to establish appropriate control systems. It must decide how best to assess the performance and control the actions of sub-units.

- *Matching strategy, structure, and controls*

  This component requires that a company achieve fit, or congruence, among its strategy, structure, and controls.

- *Managing strategic change*

  This component requires development of processes to manage strategic change and develop different tactics that managers can use to successfully implement such a change.

Once the strategic plan is in place and the above processes have been developed, an aligned technology infrastructure can be developed.

What does the preceding discussion have to do with implementing a data warehouse? The answer is *EVERYTHING!*

I found that unless I understood the corporation into which the data warehouse was to be deployed, I did not understand what and how I needed to serve the corporation.

Following are a number of additional models that were helpful in the development of our data warehouse.

A Geographic Footprint Model

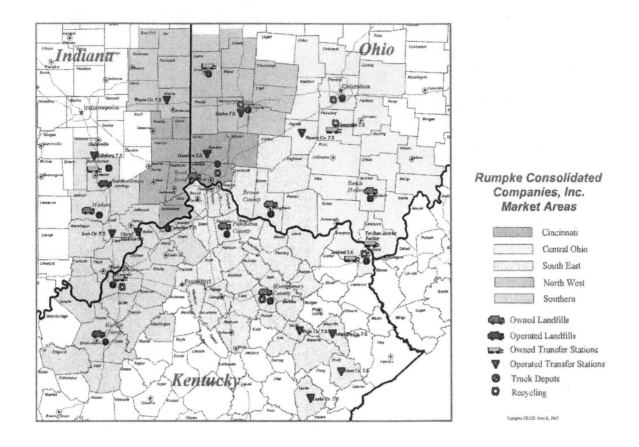

Figure 2.4

A Network Model

Rumpke Network Diagram

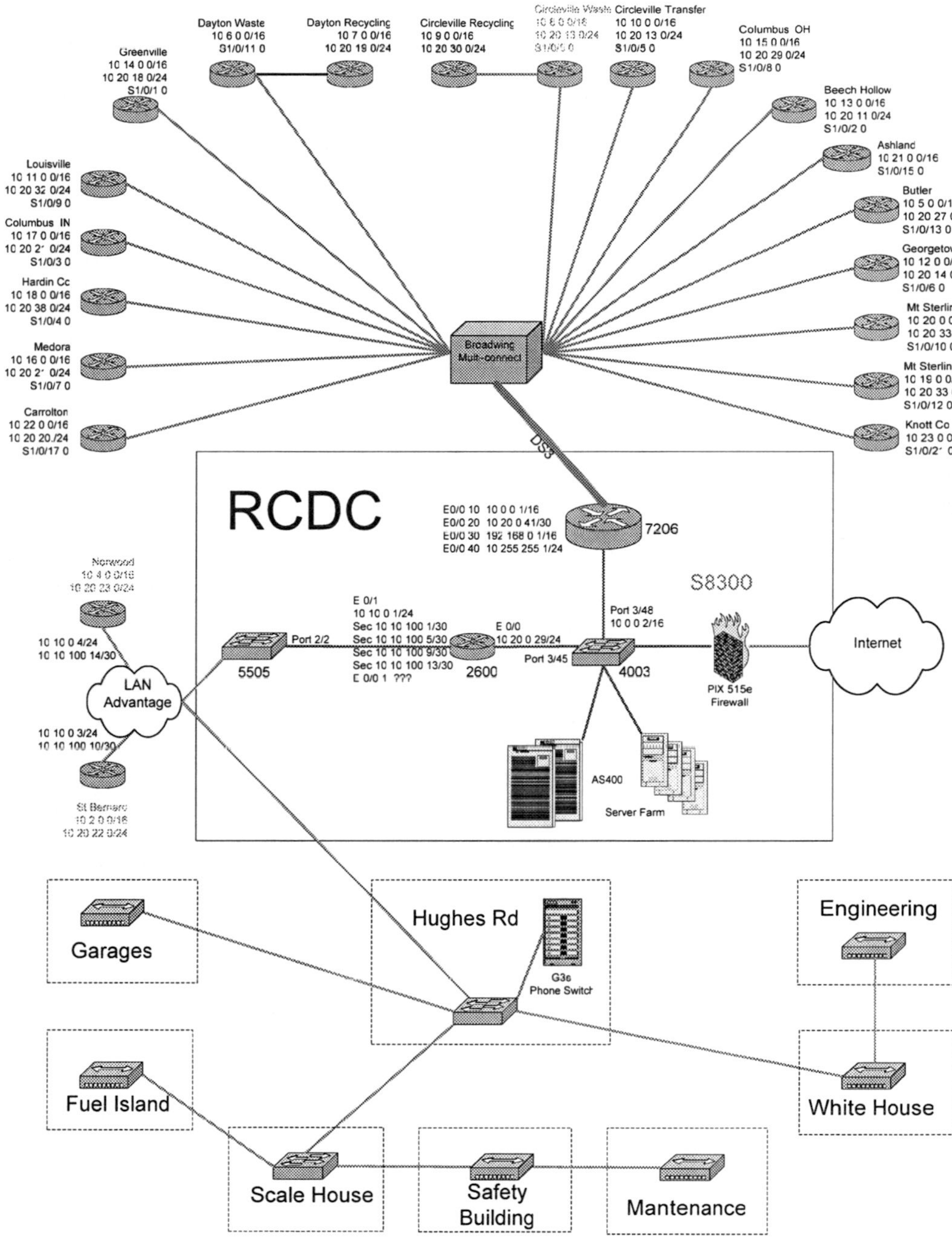

Figure 2.5

A Management Structure Model

Organizations choose an appropriate management hierarchy to meet their strategic goals. Span of control (the number of subordinates each manager manages directly) is also determined. The basic choice is whether to have a flat organizational structure with few hierarchical levels and a larger span of control, or a tall organizational structure with many hierarchical levels and smaller span of control. A data warehouse developer must model, and thoroughly understand, management structure because each organizational level will summarize information to meet the needs of their hierarchy and span of control.

Following is a management structure model showing four basic management levels:

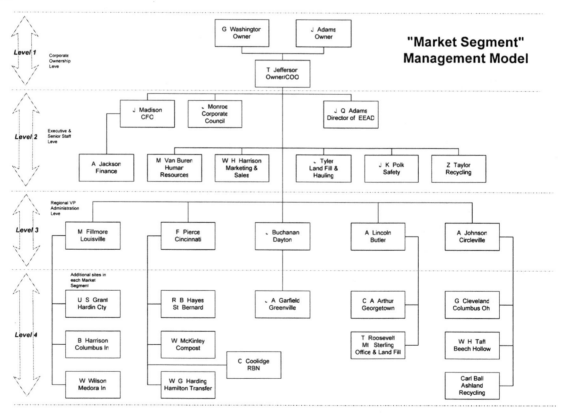

Figure 2.6

In the model shown above, the first level represents senior management and is primarily focused on organizational strategy. The second and third levels represent middle management with a primary focus on developing tactics to fit the organization strategy. The fourth level has a primary focus on implementing tactics and daily operations.

Businesses need different types of information systems to support decision making and work activity across all organizational levels. Why? Because of different interests, specialties and levels in an organization. Four main types of information systems serve different organizational levels: operational level systems, knowledge level systems, management level systems, and strategic level systems.

- *Operational level systems* support operational managers by keeping track of the elementary activities and transactions of an organization, such as sales, proceeds, cash deposits, payroll, credit decisions, and the flow of materials or services. The principal purpose of systems at this level is to answer routine questions and to track the flow of transactions through the organization.

- *Knowledge level systems* support an organization's knowledge and data workers. The purpose of these systems is to help the business integrate knowledge into the business and to help control the flow of paperwork.

- *Management level systems* serve monitoring, controlling, decision making, and administrative activities of middle managers. Management level systems are used to answer the question, "Are things working well?"

- *Strategic level systems* provide information allowing senior management to address strategic and long-term issues.

A data warehouse developer must identify management levels and the type of systems they use in order to develop an efficient and effective data warehouse.

Once the management levels within the organization are understood and the type of system being used at each level is identified and documented, the data warehouse developer can begin a series of interviews identifying specific reports that are currently used at each level. The interviewer must also learn what additional information is needed to facilitate more effective management and control at each level.

A Logical Business Model

Many companies are run by relying on years of accumulated tacit knowledge. Tacit knowledge is the expertise and experience of organizational members that have not been formally documented. Often a problem can be corrected by understanding and reengineering a process. Following is a recap of phases of process improvement.

Phases	Key Steps
Identify	A. Identify problem that cannot be solved quickly or individually. B. Identify and involve team sponsor. C. Form team and hold kickoff meeting. D. Define team objectives. E. Develop work plan (scope, steps, resources, timeline, responsibilities, etc.). F. Communicate with and involve key stakeholders throughout.
Diagnose	A. Map process. B. Further define problem. C. Identify measures and current performance. D. Perform cause analysis. E. Identify and implement quick hits. F. Continue to communicate with and involve key stakeholders throughout.
Redesign	A. Identify solutions and best practices. B. Analyze potential solutions. C. Develop and determine best solution. D. Design job level changes to support new process. E. Continue to involve and gain approval from key stakeholders.
Implement	A. Decide on, plan and conduct test. B. Evaluate test results. C. Plan and conduct full implementation. D. Measure process improvement results. E. Continue to communicate with stakeholders.
Leverage	A. Integrate changes into standard operating procedures. B. Share story and assist with wider application. C. Recognize and celebrate team results. D. Develop mechanisms for re-evaluation and continuous improvement. E. Decommission team.

Figure 2.7

You *will* come across processes begging to be reengineered. Be prepared to make that recommendation when needed. An excellent reference for beginning to understand the rationale and the art of process reengineering is *Reengineering the Corporation: A Manifesto for Business Revolution* written by Michael Hammer and James Champy.

A Logical Business Model identifies business information processes and requirements across at least four general categories. These categories of understanding are required so that a data warehouse developer can analyze process flow of business activities across the entire organization:

- The first category identifies information that must be available in order to do business. This section documents predefined information and processes required to be in place before the business can service the first customer.

- The second category identifies what the business needs to know about a customer in order to service that customer, including how customer billing is triggered and tracked.

- The third category presents the general source of both revenue and expense generation.

- The last category identifies overhead expense generation and tracking.

A Logical Data Model is independent of legacy software or hardware architecture. However, the goal of this modeling effort is to identify and understand all of the workflow processes built around information to be brought into the data warehouse.

The following diagram presents a sample Logical Business Model.

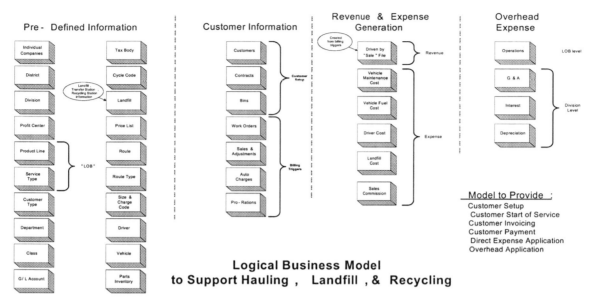

**Logical Business Model
to Support Hauling , Landfill , & Recycling**

Figure 2.8

An Operational Model

This model documents department level use of the source data being extracted to the data warehouse. The model also documents the general activity of the departments using the system. The model presents a more detailed operational view of what is needed in the data warehouse to support users of the information. The data warehouse developer will use information from this model to help determine the initial OLAP templates needed by departments using the data warehouse. The data warehouse developer will also use this information for building needed data marts.

The following diagram presents a sample Operational Model.

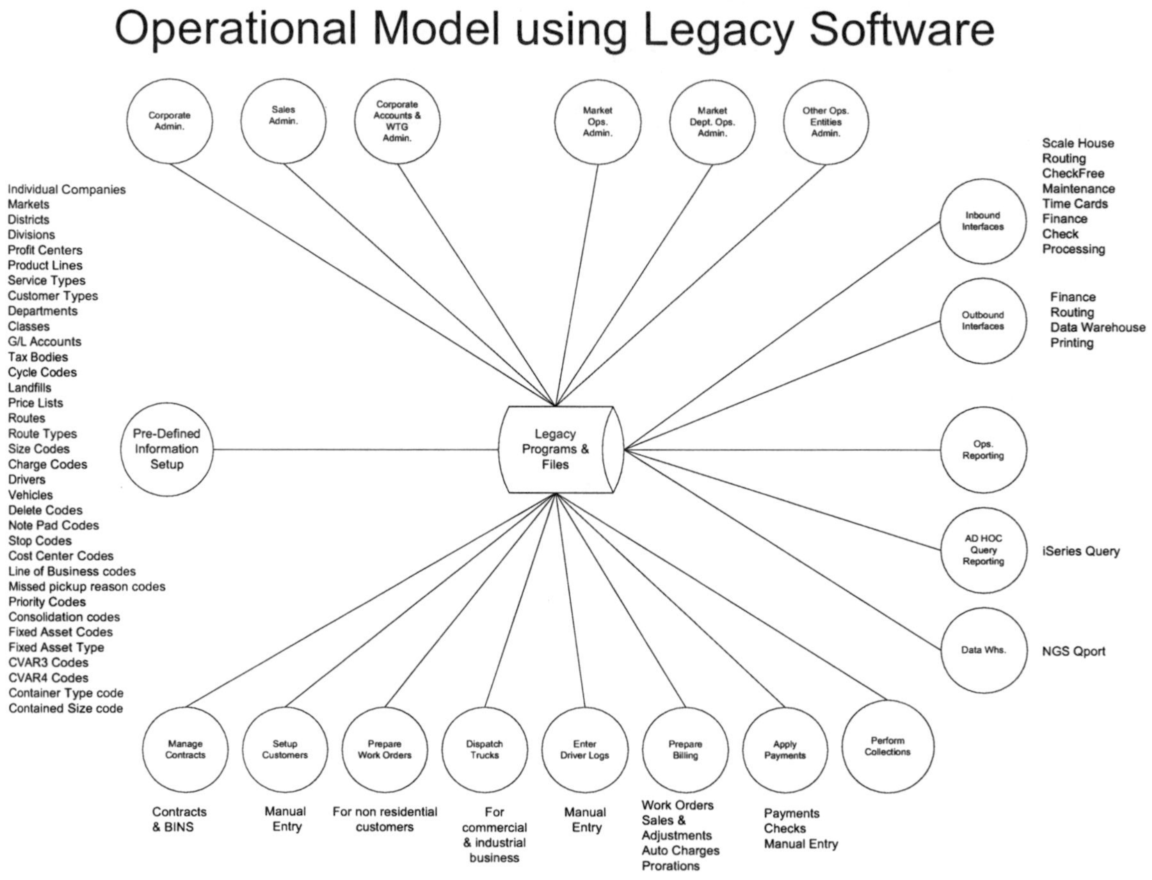

Operational Model using Legacy Software

Figure 2.9

Each activity in a department that touches or uses a legacy system should be documented at a level showing inputs, processing steps, and outputs. Again, special attention should be given to identifying any and all missing information required by the department to function successfully.

An Operations to Finance Model

This model documents the relationship between operations activity and financial reporting. The model shows how operations views and tracks activity and expenses and how that information flows into the general ledger account number structure. The example below shows the ability to track an operational activity to one driver doing one service in one truck. Company information, district or profit center information, and line of business information are moved directly to a segment of the general ledger account number, but all other operational descriptive information is lost in the financial reporting system. However, both operational level and financial level detail can be available when operational level information is moved to the data warehouse. The data warehouse developer will use this information to prepare front-end filters in data warehouse OLAP templates.

The following diagram presents a sample Operations to Finance Model.

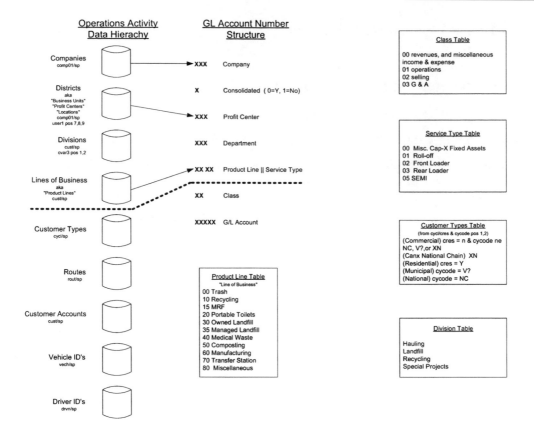

Figure 2.10

A Software Interfaces Model

This model identifies all interfaces between a company's software systems, whether external or internal. Each interface must be documented. This model is the starting point for a data warehouse developer to understand the source of information brought to the data warehouse. File and field level data sources must be understood. A data warehouse developer will use this information to help identify source data and to determine the structure of the data warehouse and data marts.

The following diagram presents a sample Software Interfaces Model:

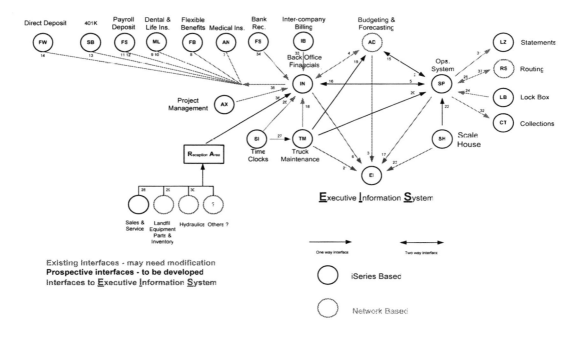

Existing & Prospective Software Interfaces Model

software interfaces vsd

Figure 2.11

Data Models

These models document file relationships within software systems. Business software systems have two general types of files: master files contain predefined information needed to support and control business activities automated by the system, and transaction files contain information identifying details of business activities as they flow though the system. This model identifies the key fields that establish the relationships between the two types of files. The first example depicts key relationships between the SoftPak transaction file SALE and other transaction and master files used by SoftPak.

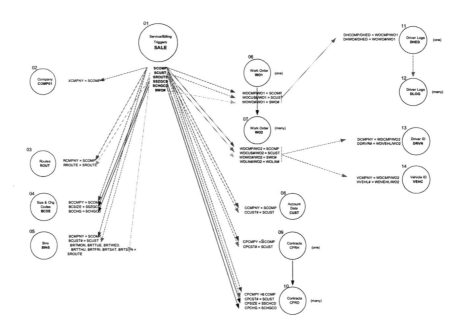

Figure 2.12

The second example depicts key relationships between the SoftPak customer master file and other supporting master and transaction files from SoftPak.

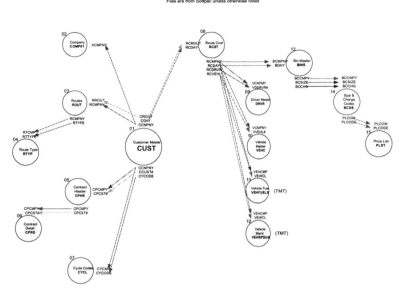

Hauling - Recycling, Residential, & Commercial Operations Data Model
- From Customer Setup to Revenue and Cost Generation -

Figure 2.13

The data warehouse developer will use these models to source data needed in the data warehouse and data marts. Once high level models are developed, they will be used to organize definition of detail data requirements, key performance indicators, critical success factors, and any other measurement metrics that will be housed in the data warehouse.

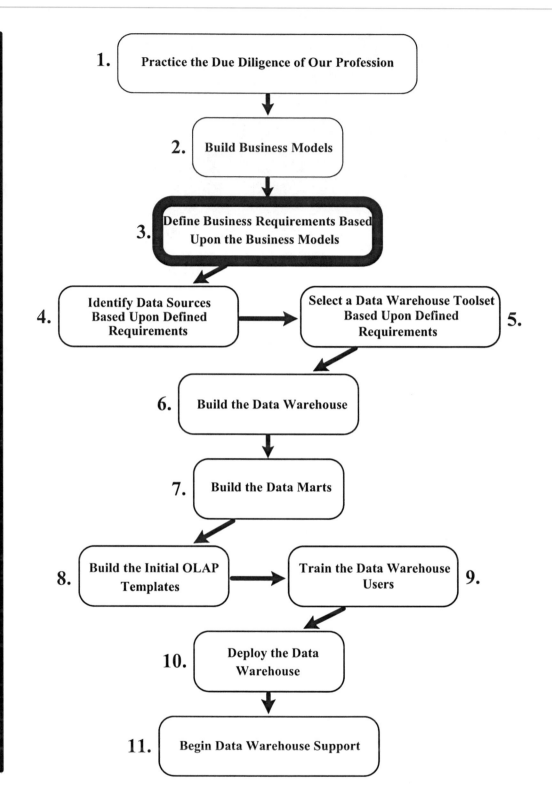

<< Data Warehouse Implementation Methodology Steps >>

1. Practice the Due Diligence of Our Profession

2. Build Business Models

3. Define Business Requirements Based Upon the Business Models

4. Identify Data Sources Based Upon Defined Requirements

5. Select a Data Warehouse Toolset Based Upon Defined Requirements

6. Build the Data Warehouse

7. Build the Data Marts

8. Build the Initial OLAP Templates

9. Train the Data Warehouse Users

10. Deploy the Data Warehouse

11. Begin Data Warehouse Support

> **"You cannot manage what you do not measure,**
> **you cannot measure what you do not track,**
> **and you cannot track what you do not plan."**
> *Anonymous*

Step 3: Define Business Requirements Based Upon the Business Models

Every business management team relies upon a set of measurements to monitor performance that determines success or failure. Two terms often used to identify these measurements are KPIs (key performance indicators) and CSFs (critical success factors). A primary purpose of the data warehouse is to prepare and present those business performance measurements. But first the performance measurements must be defined.

Many software systems do not provide adequate reporting to serve all levels of operations and management. Another primary purpose of the data warehouse is to fill that reporting capability gap. As with performance measurements, missing reports must be thoroughly defined.

Without proper definition of the expected output, a data warehouse developer will not be able to design an efficient and effective data warehouse – are the technical resources being used well, and are the customer needs being met?

The following business measurement document (page one of seven pages developed at our company) presents a view of the level of definition needed. The definition process can be long and painful. Developing consensus may be difficult indeed! However, it must be done. The data warehouse developer must have these business measurement and report definitions to determine data elements that must be present in the data warehouse. Appendix I contains a suggestion to

71

help reduce the stress while facilitating organization-wide consensus for metrics to be used (or during other steps of the methodology, for that matter).

Hauling Performance Measurements

Level of detail: Company, Route, Day, Driver, Vehicle

<u>Roll Off</u>

1. Average Revenue per Load *
   a. Revenue = all roll off hauling revenue + container lease from SoftPak (This amount contains the revenue from the work order + any additional sales within the date range selected but not derived from a work order or sales tax or intercompany moves (Charge code of IC). The additional sales amount will be split among all the customer loads for the report.)
   b. Loads = same as the productivity reports, includes all driver log entries with a service code
2. Average Hours per Load #
   a. Hours = same as productivity reports, total hours from SoftPak, excluding mechanical downtime
   b. Loads = same as the productivity reports, includes all driver log entries with a service code
3. Average Disposal Cost per Load
   a. Disposal Cost = disposal costs reported on driver log from SoftPak
   b. Load = same as the productivity reports, includes all driver log entries with a service code
4. Average Tons per Load
   a. Tons = tons reported on driver log from SoftPak (The tons of material reported from the driver log entries. The unit of measure must be entered as TN to be included in this column.)
   b. Load = same as the productivity reports, includes all driver log entries with a service code
5. Loads per Day
   a. Loads = same as the productivity reports, includes all driver log entries with a service code
   b. Day – use hours instead = same as productivity reports, total hours from SoftPak, excluding mechanical downtime
6. Loads per Month
   a. Loads = same as the productivity reports, includes all driver log entries with a service code
   b. Month = period run for the report, use total at bottom of report
7. Tons per Load   (For specific loads?)
   a. Tons = tons reported on driver log from SoftPak (The tons of material reported from the driver log entries. The unit of measure must be entered as TN to be included in this column.)
   b. Load = same as the productivity reports, includes all driver log entries with a service code
8. Disposal Costs = disposal costs reported on driver log from SoftPak
9. Truck Cost per Hour
   a. Truck Cost = (driver, payroll tax, pension, insurance from Infinium) + (truck depreciation from fixed asset system) + (labor, fuel, maintenance, wrecker, intercompany labor from TMT) + (truck leasing from Infinium – But not available at truck level) + (use tax – calculate to estimate percentage to add to fuel costs) + (insurance from Infinium (exists as total, but calculate by dividing total by number of trucks)) + (claims cost from Lotus Notes database (Accident Reporting)) + (penalty and fines from AP (Is there a field that denotes truck number?))
   b. Hours = same as productivity reports, total hours from SoftPak, excluding mechanical downtime
10. Miles Driven Daily   = miles driven in a day from SoftPak
11. Fuel – Gallons Used Daily   = TMT

SoftPak information is from DLOG, DHED, and SALE.
* Calculated on the Roll Off Profitability Report.
# Calculated on the Roll Off Productivity Report.

Last Updated: 11/19/03   Page 1

Figure 3.1

The hardest task that a business analyst has is determining what the job he or she has been given to do, in fact, really is! The beginning scope definition of a project rarely looks like the ending scope definition. The art of business analysis is arriving at the most thorough, and best, description for a given project. The data warehouse project is no different. The path to "thorough and best" follows the trail of successful user interviewing and requires skillful active listening. Our customers don't know what they know, and it is our job to find, through questioning and investigation, what they know. Following are the types of questions that need to be asked:

- What are the primary objectives of your department?
- How does your department interact with the rest of the company?
- What activities are performed daily, monthly, quarterly, and so on?
- What audits and controls are in place to measure those activities?
- What reporting tools are in place and working well today?
- What additional reporting do you need to do your job successfully?
- How do you measure success in your department?
- What constitutes failure in your department?
- Where, in the operation of your department, are you spending most of your time?
- Where are the bottlenecks in the operation of your department?
- What type of ad-hoc reporting are you typically asked to do?
- What processes are working well in your department and, conversely, what processes are not working well?
- What problem in your department would you most like to see solved?
- Does the information that your department has available meet the needs of the job?
- What historical information do you need to do your job?
- What information, forwarded to you by other departments, may be causing you problems?

- What are the red flags in your department that alert you to pending problems or trouble?
- May I have a copy of your department standard operating procedures?
- May I have a copy of your strategic plan?
- May I have a copy of the findings from the last audit of your department?

You can see by the nature of the questions that you will have to invest time and energy to determine what the data warehouse can provide. You must, as the adage says, "find the need, and fill it." Remember the Management Model. Different levels of management and supervision will have different needs.

And don't neglect the line level staff. Answers to the above questions can often bring about tremendous economies in time, money, and energy at the operational level. One particular example comes to mind. Our company processes liquid hazardous waste for disposal. The Environmental Protection Agency (EPA) requires very thorough reporting of the handling and disposal of that waste. The staff person responsible for filling out EPA reports at one of our sites was spending three to four hours a day completing the reports. Our data warehouse now gives him that information in a format accepted by the EPA. He now spends about twenty minutes a day preparing reports. We gave him back over a third of his year!

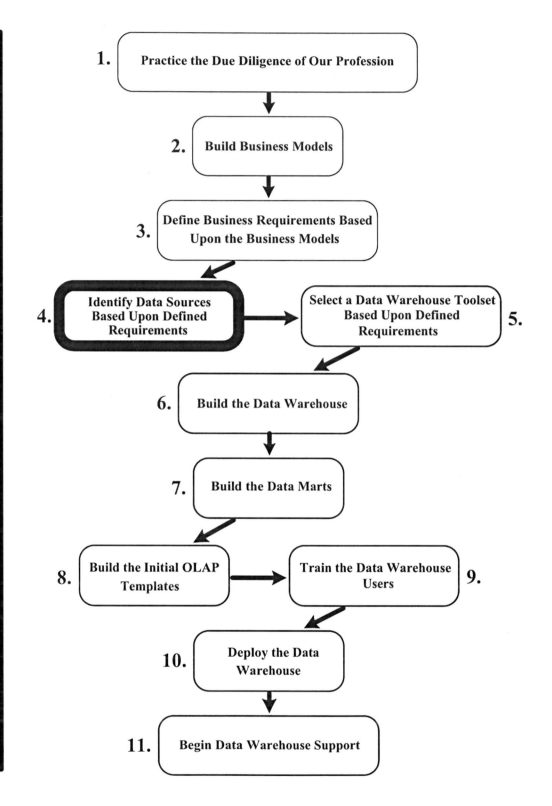

<< Data Warehouse Implementation Methodology Steps >>

1. **Practice the Due Diligence of Our Profession**

2. **Build Business Models**

3. **Define Business Requirements Based Upon the Business Models**

4. **Identify Data Sources Based Upon Defined Requirements**

5. **Select a Data Warehouse Toolset Based Upon Defined Requirements**

6. **Build the Data Warehouse**

7. **Build the Data Marts**

8. **Build the Initial OLAP Templates**

9. **Train the Data Warehouse Users**

10. **Deploy the Data Warehouse**

11. **Begin Data Warehouse Support**

> **"There is no job so simple that it cannot be done wrong."**
> *Perrussel's Law*

Step 4: Identify Data Sources Based Upon Defined Requirements

Step 2 introduced data models depicting key relationships between master file and transaction file data. Step 3 presented a sample of measurement metrics. When the work described in those steps is completed, the next step will be to expand the data models to the file/field level and identify specific data elements to be moved to the data warehouse. Information fields that will be used to select and filter record selection will also be identified. Additionally, information fields needed to derive measurement metrics must be identified and calculations documented. Needed performance measurement calculations will be performed and stored in new fields created when the extant data are moved to the data warehouse.

For example, review the SoftPak customer file key relationships diagram presented in Figure 2.9. If we wanted to bring SoftPak customer, company, and bill cycle information to the data warehouse, we would first need to identify the fields in each file. (See "Data storage hierarchy" in the Glossary.)

We will use the utility work data file (WRKDBF) to get file field descriptions for the SoftPak Customer file. EZVIEW also works well to produce this level of documentation.

On the System i command line, enter WRKDBF. Press F4 to prompt the
command.

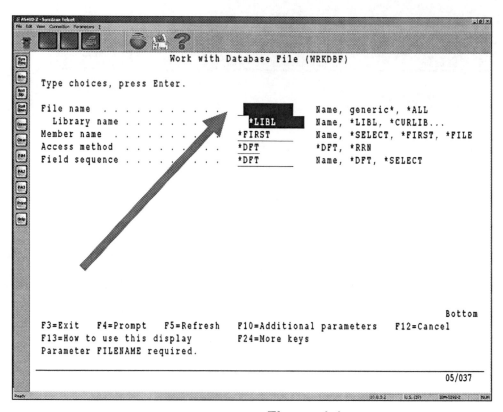

Figure 4.1

Identify Data Sources Based Upon Defined Requirements

Enter the file name and library name to access. Press Enter.

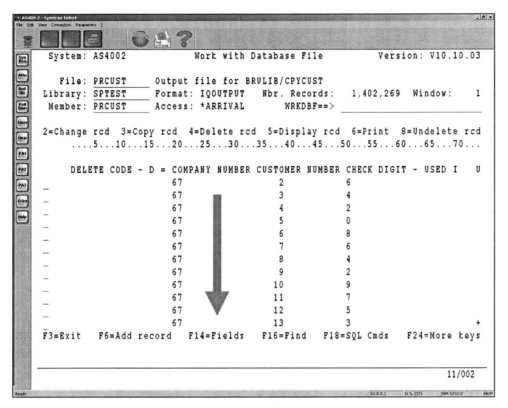

Figure 4.2

79

When the records display, press F14 to display the field sequence.

Press F21 to print a File Field Description Listing.

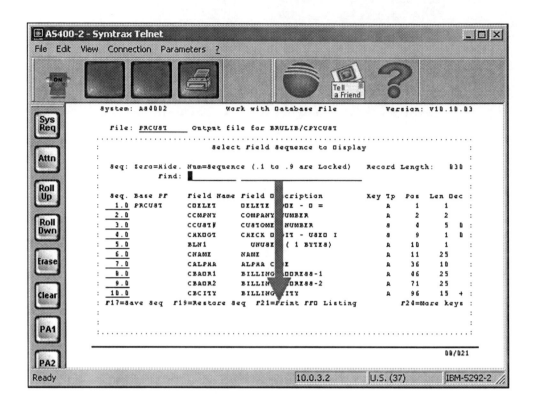

Figure 4.3

After you press F21, use WRKSPLF to find and print the listing.

First, we will get the SoftPak customer master file, page 1. (Pages 2 and 3 are not shown.)

```
Date: 10/26/05                    WRKDBF - File Field Description Listing                              Page:   1
Time: 10:59:11

    File: PRCUST    Output file for BRULIB/CPYCUST
  Library: SPTEST   Type: PF        Access: *ARRIVAL      Nbr. Formats:    1    Max. Rcdlen.:   930
   System: AS4002                                         Nbr. Fields:   137    Select/Omit?: N

Based on                                                  Key  Asc  Fld.   From    To    Fld.    Nbr.
Phys. File   Fmt. Name    Field Name   Field Description   Nbr. Dsc  Type   Pos.   Pos.   Len.    Decs.

PRCUST       IQOUTPUT     CDELET       DELETE CODE - D =              A      1      1      1
                          CCMPNY       COMPANY NUMBER                 A      2      3      2
                          CCUST#       CUSTOMER NUMBER                S      4      8      5       0
                          CHKDGT       CHECK DIGIT - USED I           S      9      9      1       0
                          BLN1            UNUSED ( 1 BYTES)           A     10     10      1
                          CNAME        NAME                           A     11     35     25
                          CALPHA       ALPHA CODE                     A     36     45     10
                          CBADR1       BILLING ADDRESS-1              A     46     70     25
                          CBADR2       BILLING ADDRESS-2              A     71     95     25
                          CBCITY       BILLING CITY                   A     96    110     15
                          CBSTAT       BILLING STATE                  A    111    112      2
                          CBZIP        BILLING ZIP                    A    113    121      9
                          CSADR1       SERVICE ADDRESS-1              A    122    146     25
                          CSADR2       SERVICE ADDRESS-2              A    147    171     25
                          CSADR3       SERVICE ADDRESS-3              A    172    196     25
                          CSCITY       SERVICE CITY                   A    197    211     15
                          CSSTAT       SERVICE STATE                  A    212    213      2
                          CSUSER       SERVICE USER                   A    214    221      8
                          CSTRET       STREET SEARCH                  A    222    236     15
                          CAREA1       PHONE NUMBER AREA CO           S    237    239      3       0
                          CPHON1       PHONE NUMBER-1                 S    240    246      7       0
                          CAREA2       PHONE NUMBER AREA CO           S    247    249      3       0
                          CPHON2       PHONE NUMBER-2                 S    250    256      7       0
                          CMSTCO       MASTER COMPANY NUMBE           A    257    258      2
                          CMSTC#       MASTER CUSTOMER NUMB           P    259    261      5       0
                          TBODY        TAX BODY                       A    262    267      6
                          ZZ3          ZZ3                            A    268    270      3
                          CSPCL1       SPECIAL INSTRUCTIONS           A    271    300     30
                          CSPCL2       SPECIAL INSTRUCTIONS           A    301    330     30
                          CSPCL3       SPECIAL INSTRUCTIONS           A    331    360     30
                          CSPCL4       SPECIAL INSTRUCTIONS           A    361    390     30
                          CCYCLE       BILLING CYCLE                  A    391    392      2
                          CSUSPN       SUSPEND CODE                   A    393    394      2
                          CSFDTE       SUSPEND FROM DATE              S    395    402      8       0
                          CSTDTE       SUSPEND TO DATE                S    403    410      8       0
                          BLN2         **UNUSED** (2 BYTES)           A    411    412      2
                          CDAY2        RECYCLING DAY                  S    413    413      1       0
                          CROUT2       RECYCLING ROUTE                A    414    415      2
                          CSEQ#2       RECYCLING ROUTE SEQU           S    416    419      4       0
                          CCFC         FINANCE CHARGES - Y/           A    420    420      1
                          CCLIMT       CREDIT LIMIT                   S    421    427      7       0
                          CCHGTP       CHANGE TYPE                    A    428    428      1
                          CUNAPL       UNAPPLIED CASH  (OPE           P    429    433      9       2
                          CVAR1        VARIABLE-1                     S    434    440      7       0
                          CVAR2        VARIABLE-2                     S    441    447      7       0
                          CVAR3        VARIABLE-3                     A    448    457     10
                          CVAR4        VARIABLE-4                     A    458    467     10
                          CCNTCT       CONTACT NAME                   A    468    492     25
```

Figure 4.4

Next, we will get field descriptions for the SoftPak Company master file.

```
Date: 10/20/05                    WRKDBF - File Field Description Listing                              Page:   1
Time: 12:01:34

    File: PRCOMP01   Output file for BRULIB/CPYCOMP01
  Library: SPTEST     Type: PF       Access: *INDEXED     Nbr. Formats:    1    Max. Rcdlen.:    37
   System: AS4002     Maint: *IMMED  Unique?: N            Nbr. Fields:    3    Select/Omit?: N

Based on                                                  Key  Asc  Fld.   From    To    Fld.    Nbr.
Phys. File   Fmt. Name    Field Name   Field Description   Nbr. Dsc  Type   Pos.   Pos.   Len.    Decs.

PRCOMP01     IQOUTPUT     XCMPNY       COMPANY NUMBER       1    A    A      1      2      2
                          XNAME        NAME                           A      3     27     25
                          XUSR1        USER DEFINED FIELD -           A     28     37     10
```

Figure 4.5

Finally, we will get field descriptions for the SoftPak bill cycle master file.

```
Date: 10/20/05                    WRKDBF - File Field Description Listing                        Page:   1
Time: 12:11:24

    File: PRCYCL       Output file for BRULIB/CPYCYCL
 Library: SPTEST       Type: PF        Access: *ARRIVAL      Nbr. Formats:    1     Max. Rcdlen.:   552
  System: AS4002                                             Nbr. Fields:    69     Select/Omit?:  N

Based on                                                 Key   Asc   Fld.    From    To    Fld.   Nbr.
Phys. File    Fmt. Name    Field Name    Field Description  Nbr.  Dsc   Type    Pos.   Pos.   Len.   Decs.

PRCYCL        IQOUTPUT     CYDELT        DELETE CODE -D w R               A      1      1      1
                          CRECID        RECID = Y                        A      2      2      1
                          CYCMP         COMPANY NUMBER                   A      3      4      2
                          CYCODE        CYCLE CODE                       A      5      6      2
                          BLNK6           UNUSED ( 6 BYTES)              A      7     12      6
                          BLNK5           UNUSED ( 5 BYTES)              A     13     17      5
                          CYDSC1        CYCLE DESCRIPTION-1              A     18     42     25
                          CYDSC2        CYCLE DESCRIPTION-2              A     43     67     25
                          CYMULT        CYCLE MULTIPLIER                 S     68     69      2      0
                          CYRES         RESIDENTIAL CUSTOMER             A     70     70      1
                          CYDEFR        DEFER G/L REPORTING              S     71     72      2      0
                          CGLCOD        A/R GL CODE (ABBREVI             A     73     77      5
                          CPRDYS        CPRDYS                           S     78     80      3      0
                          BLNK17        BLNK17                           A     81     97     17
                          CFINCE        FINANCE CHARGE PERCE             S     98    101      4      4
                          CMNBAL        FINANCE MINIMUM BALA             S    102    105      4      0
                          CRTECD        ROUTE CARDS - Y/N                A    106    106      1
                          CBILNG        AUTOMATIC BILLING? -             A    107    107      1
                          CFCHGS        FINANCE CHARGES - Y/             A    108    108      1
                          CFGLCD        FINANCE CHARGE GENER             A    109    113      5
                          CYFCMN        FINANCE CHARGE MINIM             S    114    117      4      2
                          CYFCAT        FINANCE CHARGE AT...             S    118    119      2      0
                          BLNK14        **UNUSED**                       A    120    133     14
                          CBILIN        BILL BIN INVENTORY?              A    134    134      1
                          CBORC         BAL. FWD OR OPEN ITE             A    135    135      1
                          CWOWL         DEFAULT WORK ORDER O             A    136    136      1
                          CWOYN         DEFAULT PRINT INVOIC             A    137    137      1
                          CWODT         DEFAULT DETAIL OR TO             A    138    138      1
                          CWAGE1        AGE HEADING OVERRIDE             A    139    148     10
                          CWAGE2        AGE HEADING OVERRIDE             A    149    158     10
                          CWAGE3        AGE HEADING OVERRIDE             A    159    168     10
                          CWAGE4        AGE HEADING OVERRIDE             A    169    178     10
                          CEOMDT        LAST MONTH END DATE              S    179    186      8      0
                          CEOMTM        LAST MONTH END TIME              S    187    194      8      0
                          BLANK8        UNUSED                           A    195    202      8
                          BLANK2        UNUSED                           A    203    204      2
                          CEOMBA        LAST END OF MONTH BI             A    205    205      1
                          CEOMST        LAST END OF MONTH ST             A    206    206      1
                          CEOMAG        LAST END OF MONTH AG             A    207    207      1
                          CBADAT        DATE AUTO BILLED LAS             A    208    215      8
                          CSTDAT        DATE STMT PRINTED LA             A    216    223      8
                          CAGDAT        DATE AGED LAST                   A    224    231      8
                          CCNTPR        CONTRACT PRICING REQ             A    232    232      1
                          CACLAS        ACCOUNT CLASSIFICATI             A    233    233      1
                          CATB          INCLUDE THIS CYCLE I             A    234    234      1
                          BLNK8         UNUSED                           A    235    242      8
                          BLK8          UNUSED                           A    243    250      8
                          CPRTY         PRIORITY (WO DEFAULT             A    251    251      1
```

Figure 4.6

Now that we have field descriptions, we can select the fields that we want to move to the data warehouse. Remember to include needed numeric fields as well as fields that will be used later to filter records. In addition, we want to make sure that we have all extant data needed for the derived calculations we identified as measurement metrics. Try to create derived data fields in the Copy, Build, and Load processes as early as possible. If you don't, you may have to create them over and over again! (See Appendix F for a lesson learned!)

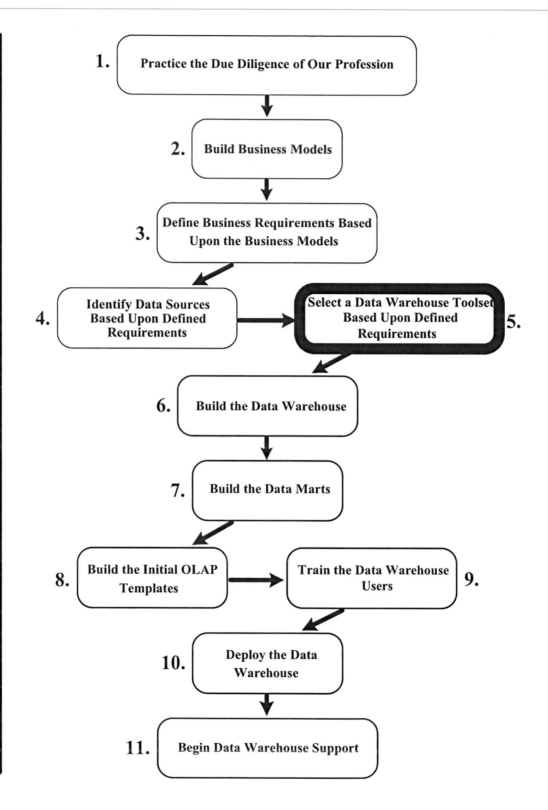

<< Data Warehouse Implementation Methodology Steps >>

1. Practice the Due Diligence of Our Profession

2. Build Business Models

3. Define Business Requirements Based Upon the Business Models

4. Identify Data Sources Based Upon Defined Requirements

5. Select a Data Warehouse Toolset Based Upon Defined Requirements

6. Build the Data Warehouse

7. Build the Data Marts

8. Build the Initial OLAP Templates

9. Train the Data Warehouse Users

10. Deploy the Data Warehouse

11. Begin Data Warehouse Support

> **"It has long come to my attention that people of accomplishment
> rarely sat back and let things happen to them.
> They went out and happened to things."**
> *Leonardo da Vinci*

Step 5: Select a Data Warehouse Toolset Based Upon Defined Requirements

In the previous steps, we determined the work tools that we would use to manage our data warehouse implementation project. We modeled the business, we determined what we wanted the data warehouse to measure, we developed a set of business rules and requirements, and then we identified the sources of data. We also identified existing fields we would need and then defined derived data. We have completed phase 3 of our traditional SDLC model. And we determined to move forward with the project. We are ready to organize and present our information to data warehouse toolset vendors.

We determined in Step 1 that we would use an RFP format to document our findings. However, the consulting world would have us prepare a document that is often onerous and over-engineered, giving vendors a difficult time determining what we really want, and us in identifying the vendors that can do it! So we need to simplify the RFP format.

Again, we need to eliminate sizzle and provide substance. Documentation created thus far will be the source of the substance in our RFP. To that substance we will need to add a few housekeeping rules for vendors to follow during the RFP process. Our RFP document should contain, at a minimum, the following:

1.   A narrative of what we're trying to accomplish with a data warehouse.
2.   The models of our business.

3. Descriptions of the legacy systems containing the source data for the data warehouse.

4. Descriptions of the hardware environment and technology infrastructure currently used.

5. A matrix of required data warehouse toolset function:

    - A variety of user interfaces to support analysis, presentation and reporting needs of technical staff, power users, and non-technical users.

    - Ability to have queries saved and run with a simple click of a desktop icon, allowing technical and non-technical end users the ability to produce updated reports, on-screen views, file downloads, etc. quickly and easily from predefined query definitions.

    - Provide a Web-based dashboard interface that allows administrative, technical, and even novice end users with point-and-click access to high-level business performance information with drill-down capability where appropriate.

    - Online analytical processing and multi-dimensional presentation interface to support easy analysis at the desktop.

    - Ability to load query output into Microsoft Office (Excel, Access, and Word) applications to support analysis and presentation.

    - Ability to update/refresh Excel workbooks and sheets while preserving formatting, formulas and other existing design elements in the file.

    - Provide a Windows and/or Web-browser graphical interface that helps users design develop reports quickly and easily.

    - Support the use of existing queries as templates for new ones.

    - Support inner, outer and exception file joins, joins based on calculated fields, and one-to-many joins to simplify complex query development.

    - Provide facility for an administrator to predefine file join relationships to shield end users from the complexity of the underlying database when building queries.

    - Provide facility for establishing alias names for files and fields to make the database easier for users to understand.

- Support simple and compound record selection logic with the option for query to prompt the user at run time for variable criteria.
- Support run-time prompting on calculated fields to enable users to customize how a field should be computed.
- Allow for easy reformatting of date fields to improve presentation, sorting or calculation processes.
- Support an extensive list of date arithmetic functions – days between dates, use of system date in calculations, elapsed days, etc.
- Support the definition of new fields based on multiple IF-THEN rules so as to simplify the development of "bucket" reports and reduce the need for running multiple queries before obtaining a final report.
- Ability to calculate running totals, percentage of group totals, averages, ranks and other summary values.
- Ability to use summary totals generated in the query in additional calculations without the need to output a summary work file.
- Provide a facility for designing the report layout.
- Provide a method for integrating customer-supplied programs with the query processing routine so that special processing needs such as encryption or complex calculations can be included in the query execution process.
- Support the linking of queries for sequential execution so that custom query runs can be easily defined without programmer intervention.
- The ability to generate Web reports with drillable hypertext links to support point-and-click navigation through multiple levels of summary and detail output.
- Support the creation of detail and summary DB2 UDB output files, with or without key fields.
- Offer integrated e-mail and FTP functions for directing output to multiple locations in formats such as PDF, CSV, TXT, HTML, and XML.
- Ability to schedule queries for execution using IBM and third-party job scheduling software.

- Ability to call defined queries or reports from within CL programs.
- Ability to pass parameters to a query or report at run time.
- Ability to generate audit trails showing what queries have been revised/run, who revised/ran them, what date they were revised/run, what files were accessed, how much time was required to process the request, and other useful information to assist with scheduling, performance tuning, compliance, and security.
- Support the ability to issue a command function to change the data library and/or files associated with a query.
- Able to operate in complete accordance with i5/OS security standards at all levels.
- File or data accessibility based on standard operating system security.
- Ability to secure data access at the file, field and record level by user profile.
- Ability to secure queries so only authorized users can modify and run them.
- Ability to secure queries so only authorized users can distribute output as an attachment to an e-mail message.

6. Vendor presentation ground rules – how we want to see the prospective vendor solutions presented.
7. Financial terms and conditions.

Finding Data Warehouse or Business Intelligence Product Vendors

There are many of sources for identifying vendors that might meet the needs of the data warehouse for your size company. Although there are too many vendors to list here and the list changes constantly, here are some suggestions to get you pointed in the right direction:

- Call your peers. Listen to what they have already done and the problems they may have encountered.
- Look at DM-review.com and TWDI.org.
- Do an Internet search on DW 2.0.
- Read anything and everything by Bill Inmon, Dr. Ralph Kimball, Gloria Imhoff, or Mike Cain – they are among the acknowledged leaders and visionaries of data warehouse and business intelligence.
- Attend the next COMMON conference (or just look at the vendors present at the last conference). Many data warehouse or business intelligence System i vendors will have a booth!
- Read the IDC "Competitive Analysis" (July 2006) of business intelligence tool vendors.
- Review *System iNEWS* for System i toolsets (systeminetwork.com).
- Review *IBM Systems Magazine* for System i data warehouse toolsets.
- If all else fails – many consultants will be happy to help you part with your money.

Remember the goal – to find the best toolset match for your requirements and within your budget (resist the temptation to develop the toolset in-house) and move forward with the project.

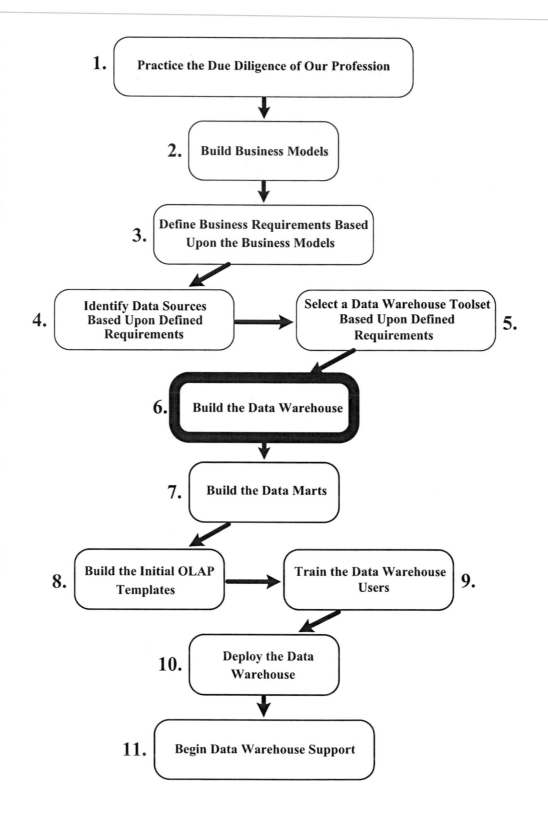

<< Data Warehouse Implementation Methodology Steps >>

1. Practice the Due Diligence of Our Profession

2. Build Business Models

3. Define Business Requirements Based Upon the Business Models

4. Identify Data Sources Based Upon Defined Requirements

5. Select a Data Warehouse Toolset Based Upon Defined Requirements

6. Build the Data Warehouse

7. Build the Data Marts

8. Build the Initial OLAP Templates

9. Train the Data Warehouse Users

10. Deploy the Data Warehouse

11. Begin Data Warehouse Support

"Everything can look like a failure in the middle!"
Kanter's Law

Step 6: <u>Build the Data Warehouse</u>

Overview

Now that steps 1 through 4 are complete and we have a data warehouse and business intelligence toolset in place (Step 5), we can begin constructing the data warehouse. The following diagram illustrates how that will happen:

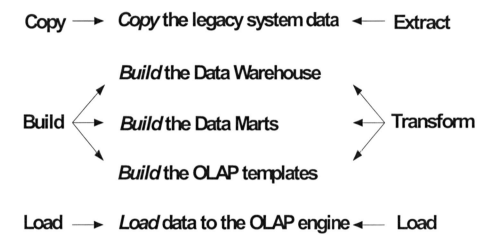

Figure 6.1

For our purposes here, I have chosen to define the process using the terms "copy," "build," and "load." Technology professionals often use the terms "extract," "transform," and "load." But because reading and research has shown such definition diversity and, in my judgment, created much confusion, I have chosen not to use the terms "extract," "transform," and "load."

Having said that, the following is quoted from Dr. Ralph Kimball's comprehensive work titled, *The Data Warehouse Lifecycle Toolkit*:

> Data staging is a major process that includes, among others, the following sub-processes: extracting, transforming, loading and indexing, and quality assurance checking. The extract step is the first step of getting data into the data warehouse environment. We use this term more narrowly then some consultants. Extracting means reading and understanding the source data, and *copying* the parts that are needed to the data staging area for further work.

Copy, build, and load processes relate to our two-tiered data warehouse model as follows:

Build the Data Warehouse

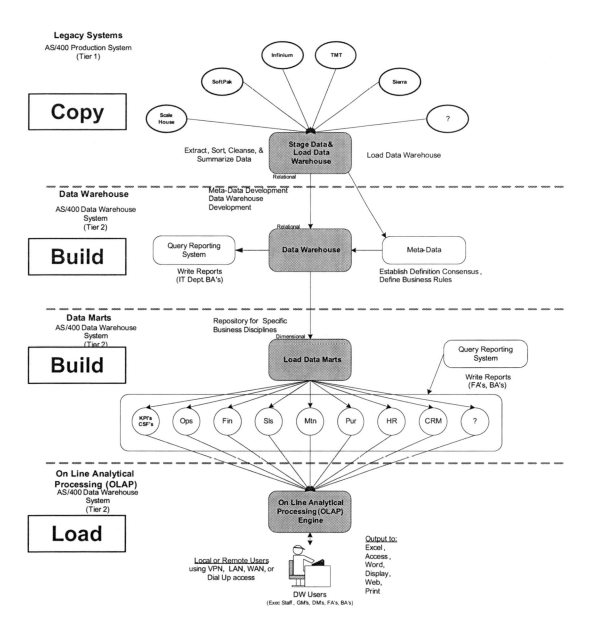

Figure 6.2

COPY - Copying the Legacy System Data

Earlier in the methodology discussion, we decided that we wanted, among other things, customer information as well as associated company and bill cycle information moved to the data warehouse. We identified extant data elements and defined derived information, and we documented performance measurement metrics needed to manage the business. Now, we will begin to copy that sourced information to the data warehouse. Our chosen files strategy is to use a flat file architecture within the data warehouse instead of retaining the dimensional architecture of the legacy system currently holding customer information. What worked best for our company was a combination of the dimensional and flat file architecture.

The diagram below illustrates how to establish key relationships between a sales transaction file and a number of associated master files. We use the company number, the customer number, and the billing cycle identification to establish the "many to one" relationship. When the relationships are established, a record can be written to the data warehouse staging area. This record can contain field names and data from the sales transaction file as well as the related master files. Building a flat file at the staging process greatly simplifies handling legacy data as meta data is designed, records are cleansed (don't forget to return the cleansed data to the legacy system), the data warehouse is built, and data marts are prepared.

This following diagram depicts building an output flat file from dimensional legacy files that have a "many to one" relationship.

A Dimensional to Flat File Data Model
Using meta-data field names

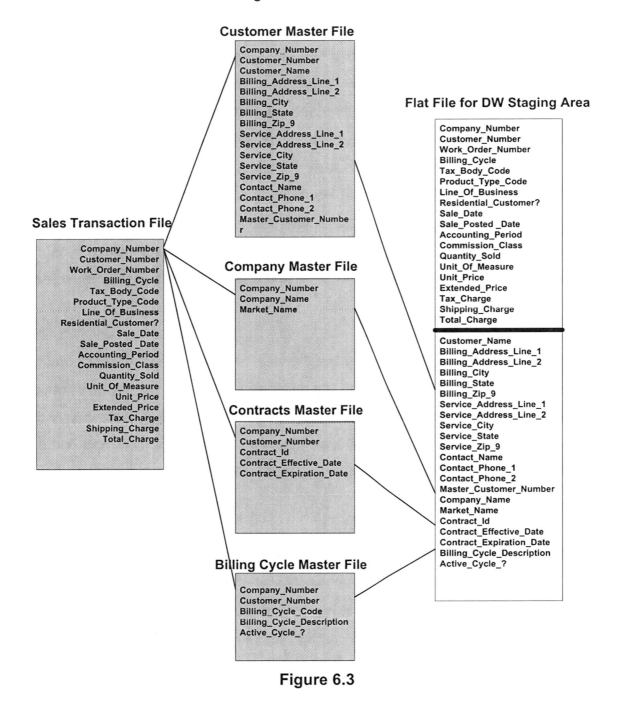

Figure 6.3

Using this model, we will read a sales transaction record, find the associated

customer, company, contract, and bill cycle records, and then write one record to the staging area containing selected fields from all the files related to the sale transaction. A little bit of file theory is in order here.

Joining Files – One to One

Our data warehouse toolset (NGS-IQ™) query function allows us to join files by key fields and write specific fields we select to an output file. We had to decide how to join the files and then select the fields we wanted in our output file. We used the customer master, the company master, and the bill cycle master. We will also have to decide if we want to copy all of the customer records or just a subset of the records. For example, we may want active customers only or, perhaps, just customers for a certain line of business. Alternatively, we might want to copy all the active and inactive customers to the data warehouse staging area, create a data warehouse containing all the records, and create data marts later for selected customer subsets.

We know we can match (join) a customer master file record to the corresponding company master file record by using the **company** field from the customer master file to match with the **company** field in the company master file. There is only one company associated with each customer. So, our copy function can read each customer master file record and find the company to which the customer is assigned.

We also know we can match a customer master record to the corresponding bill cycle master file record by joining on the company and bill cycle fields from each file. If we wanted to join more files to the customer master, we could do so by finding matching fields in both files. Master files (sometimes called dimension tables) typically have a one-to-one relationship with other master files.

Joining Files – Many to One

Transaction files (sometimes called fact tables) often have a many-to-one relationship with master files. For instance, our legacy system contains a file with multiple years of sales transactions. We can easily extract sale records by date range and match the customer number field in the sale record to the corresponding customer number in the customer master file. Each sale record can be joined with a corresponding customer master record, and information from both records can be written to our sale transaction flat file in the data warehouse, as described above.

Moving Ahead with Copying Data

Our planning is completed and we are ready to write the query that creates a data file. We will store the resulting output file in a staging location to be used later when we build the data warehouse file.

But first, a graphical representation of creating a flat file data warehouse record from input organized dimensionally in a legacy system.

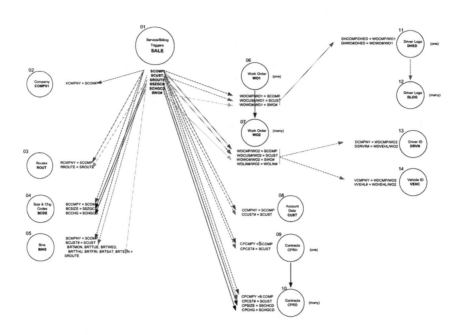

Figure 6.4

During Step 2 of the methodology, we developed a dimensional model showing relationships between the transaction file containing one record for each sale activity and the supporting master files from which further details associated with each sale can be accessed. We will begin building our flat file by reading a sale transaction record. We will then perform joins with the associated customer record, company record, routing record, work order header record, and customer contract record. Based upon the metrics our customers wanted to see in the data warehouse (Step 3 of the methodology), we will select fields from each of the specific joined records to include in the data warehouse staging record. The staging area sales record will be organized with sale transaction detail fields followed by selected customer record fields, company record fields, routing fields, work order header fields, and finally, customer contract information.

The flat file record will, in effect, be a concatenation of fields from a number of different files. Review figure 6.3.

Before we move on to actually building a data warehouse file, we need to address two issues: meta data and data cleansing.

Using Meta Data (Data about Our Data)

For our purposes here, we will define meta data as the ability to create a virtual file in which we can assign different English-like names to existing files and fields, including derived data fields. We can replace cryptic names, typically used by programmers when creating a file and its structure, with meaningful names for the files and fields we are using in the data warehouse.

What is the major benefit of meta data?

Meta data allows us to present meaningful names to our users when we filter and present records using the OLAP engine. The following table shows cryptic names followed by meta data names for fields available in the sales data mart. Blank cryptic name entries represent derived data. This table was placed in the data warehouse user manual.

Cryptic Name	Expanded Name	Data Element Description
	ABCD_CODE	ABCD Analysis Code – TYPSRC position 4
	BCYCLEPOS1	First position of the Bill Cycle code
	CONTACT_NAME	Customer contact name
	CUST_SORT_NAME	Customer sort name
	DAYS_OLD	Customer age in days
	DAYSTOEOC	Day to the contract end date (from TODAYSDAT)
	DEFAULT_ROUTE	Soft-Pak default route
	DISTRICT_CODE	District Code – cross reference file
	DISTRICT_NAME	District Name – cross reference file
	FS_PERCENT	Fuel Surcharge percent from CVAR2
	FUEL_CHARG	Position seven of TYPSRC – customer exempt from fuel surcharge
	LOB_TYPE	Positions 1 and 2 of TYPSRC – Service Type code
	MARKET_NAME	Market Name – cross reference file
	MASTER_CO_NO	Master Company Number
	MASTER_CUST_NO	Master customer number
	MUN_ACCT#	Municipal account number

Cryptic Name	Expanded Name	Data Element Description
	PERM_TEMP	Position 3 of TYPSRC – permanent or temporary customer
	PLIST_POS1	First position of the Price List code
	PREV_CYCLE	Previous bill cycle
	PRICE_CODE	Positions 5 and 6 of TYPSRC – Sale Price code
	RCYHAUL	SCHGCD pos 1, length 1
	RCYSALE	SSCGCD pos 2, length 1
	RESCODE	Soft-Pak – CPLIST , pos 1, length 1
	RLFLCODE	Soft-Pak CVAR3, pos 1, length 2
	SALEPRSN	Sales person associated with a sale. From Soft-Pak SVAR4, pos 1, length 3
	SALES_PERSON	Sales person initials from CVAR4
	SALESINIT	Sales person associated with a customer. From Soft-Pak CVAR4, pos 1, length 3
	SIZ_CHG_1	Four character size and charge code position 1
	SIZ_CHG_2	Four character size and charge code position 2
	SIZ_CHG_3	Four character size and charge code position 3
	SIZ_CHG_4	Four character size and charge code position 4
	STREET_SEARCH	Street name search
	SVTYPE	GLGL pos 7, length 2
	TODAYSDAT	Date the Qport output was created
	TXBODYPOS1	First position for the Tax Body code
	ZIP_CODE_5	First five positions of the service zip code
	ZIP5	CSZIP, pos 1, length 5
BBILL$	REGULAR_CHARGE	BINS – Amount to be billed
BBIN#	BIN_SEQ_NUMBER	BINS – bin sequence number
BCDESC		BCDE – Bin Description
BQTY		BINS – Quantity of BINS
BTOTPU	WEEKLY_PICKUPS	BINS – number of weekly pickups
BUSTYPE	LOB_TYPE	SVAR3, pos 1, length 2
CCYCLE	BILL_CYCLE	Soft-Pak – billing cycle code
CMTH$	MONTHLY_CHARGE	Monthly service charge
CNAME	CUSTOMER_NAME	Soft-Pak customer name
CNAT#	NATIONAL_ACC#	National account number
CPCONT	CONTRACT_ID	Soft-Pak contract number
CPEFDT	EFFECTIVE_DATE	Soft-Pak contract effective date
CPEXDT	EXPIRE_DATE	Soft-Pak contract expiration date
CPLIST	PRIC_LIST_CODE	Soft-Pak - Price list code
CRES	RES_CUSTOMER	Soft-Pak – residential customer code
CROUT1	RES_ROUTE	Soft-Pak – residential customer route
CSCITY	SERVICE_CITY	Service City
CSSTAT	SERVICE_STATE	Service Sate
CSTDTE	START_DATE	Soft-Pak customer service start date
CSTOP	STOP_DATE	Soft-Pak customer stop date
CSTRDT	START_DATE	Soft-Pak – customer start date
CSZIP	SERV_ADD_ZIP	Full service address zip code
CVAR3	TYPSRC	TYPSRC code
DPPRTY		Priority Code
DPTRUK		Vehicle ID
GLCMPY	GL_COMPANY	Infinium company code
GLDESC1	GL_DESC_1	Soft-Pak general ledger account description 1
GLGL	GL_NUMBER	Soft-Pak actual GL posting account number
MKTCC	PROFIT_CENTER	Profit Center – cross reference file
NCODE		Note Pad Code (for lost business reason)
NNOTE		Note Pad Text
NUPDATE		Note Pad date updated

Cryptic Name	Expanded Name	Data Element Description
PLDESC	PIRCE_LIST_DESC	Price List Description
RCDCNT	RCD_COUNT	Used to provide counts of selected records
RCDRVH		Driver Hours
RCDRVR		Driver ID
RCREV$		Revenue
SCCHG	CHARGE_CODE	Charge type from SALE file
SCOMP	COMPANY_ID	Soft-Pak company code
SCUST	CUSTOMER_NBR	Soft-Pak customer number
SCYCL	BILLCYCL	Soft-Pak billing cycle
SDATE	DATE_POSTED	Soft-Pak date representing when a sale is posted to Soft-Pak. An 8 position date in CCYYMMDD format
SDESC	SALE_DESCRIPTN	Soft-Pak sale description
SGLCD	GLCODE	Soft-Pak 5 character G/L posting code
SHGGCD	CHRGCODE	Soft-Pak charge code
SQTY	QUANTITY	Soft-Pak SALE file quantity
SSGCDE	SIZE_CODE	Soft-Pak size code
STAX		Tax record from SALE file
STOT	AMOUNT_BILLED	Soft-Pak billing amount
STOTSM		STOT sub-total
SVTYPE	SERVTYPE	Soft-Pak service type GLGL, pos 7, length 2
TBCNDS	COUNTY_DESC	Tax Body County Description
TBCNTY	COUNTY_CODE	Tax Body County code
TBCODE	TAX_BODY_CODE	Tax Body Code
TBSTAT	STATE_CODE	Tax Body State
TBTWDS	TOWNSHIP_DESC	Tax Body Township Description
TBTWSP	TOWNSHIP_CODE	Tax Body Township code
WO#	WORKORD#	Soft-Pak work order number
WOADAT		Work order action date
WOCMP		Work Order company
WOCUS#		Work Order Customer Number
WOROUT		Work Order Route
WOWO#	WORK_ORDER_NBR	Work Order number
XNAME	COMPANY_DESC	Soft-Pak company name
YRMTH	YEAR_AND_MONTH	4 digit number representing a year/month combination. e.g:0401 represents January, 2004. The leading zero is optional

Figure 6.5

In a December 2005 paper entitled "The Influence of End-User Metadata on User Attitudes Toward, and Use of, a Data Warehouse" written by Neil Foshay, Assistant Professor at Saint Francis Xavier University, the author hypothesized that:

- End-user meta data quality and use have a positive impact on user attitudes toward the data in their data warehouse

101

- User attitudes influence user perception of both the usefulness and ease of use of the data warehouse
- User perception of ease of use and usefulness of the data warehouse influence the level of use of the data warehouse

This study concluded that:

> …results support these hypotheses. Implications of the study results are significant for data warehouse practitioners….The study indicates that users perceive the value of meta data and suggests that there's a tremendous opportunity for practitioners to encourage increased levels of adoption and use of their data warehouses, particularly among new data warehouse users, by implementing effective meta data and integrating it into quality and training programs.

Meta Data Lessons Learned

- Use meta data at the beginning of the project. Meta data names make training users and data filtering much, much easier!
- Create derived data fields very early in the copy or build process. Otherwise, you may have to recreate the fields many times later downstream! For example, LDSALES (see Appendix F) has a number of user-defined fields that should have been created during the copy or build process!

Look at the following examples to see why we will use meta data. Examples are shown using NGS-IQ™.

The following panel contains a sample of field names from the legacy system sale transaction file.

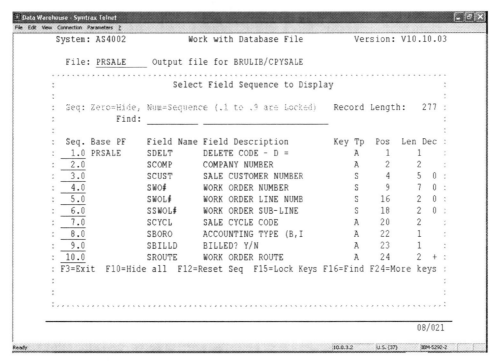

Figure 6.6

Here are the some of the meta data field names for that same file. Notice that both the file name and the field names have been changed.

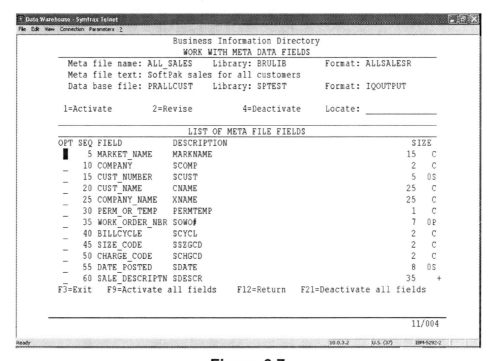

Figure 6.7

Therefore, the OLAP engine that would have presented these cryptic field names to our users:

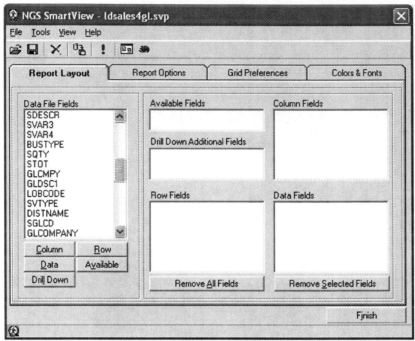

Figure 6.8

Can now present meaningful names:

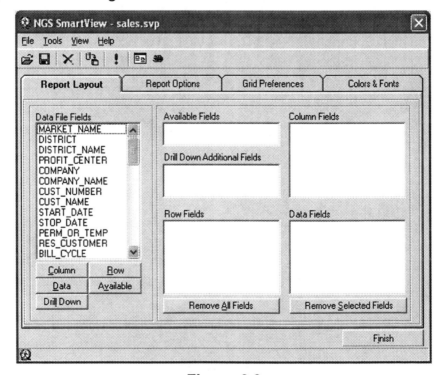

Figure 6.9

Data Cleansing

Data cleansing is correcting errors and inconsistencies in data to increase accuracy so that data can be used in a standard, company-wide format (Laudon & Laudon 2002).

Data cleansing is a core requirement of data warehousing and begins with a data quality audit. A data quality audit is a structured survey of files for accuracy and completeness. Without data cleansing, OLAP selection filters may not successfully include all desired information. In our company, operational and customer service managers were asked to define business rules associated with what were, in their judgment, key data elements. A set of data quality audits was then added to the OLAP tool to validate application of the business rules that were defined. Responsible line level managers can run the validation audits anytime they like to verify the integrity of their data and assure that the data fits the business rules. Senior management also can run the validation audits to ensure that the operational and customer service managers are doing their jobs. Maintaining data integrity has thereby been demystified and made visible. Data integrity audit results are now a part of each monthly operations review (MOR). There are no more excuses for operational data outside of the business rules.

The following are examples showing the need for data cleansing from our experience. The first example shows improper spelling of a city name in the legacy customer file.

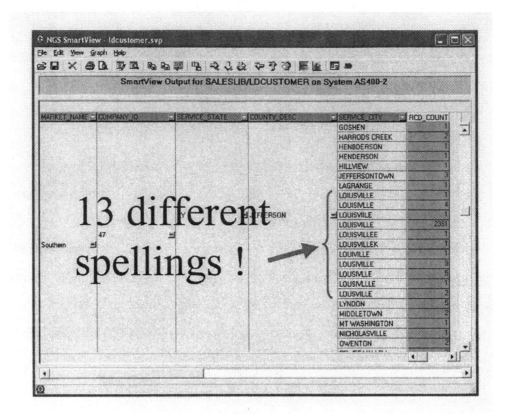

Figure 6.10

If a data warehouse user wanted to select customer records for the city of Louisville, they would miss 26 customers!

The second example shows an inconsistent entry of zip codes. Some zip codes are blank, some have five digits, some have nine digits, one is all zeros, and one has a leading blank.

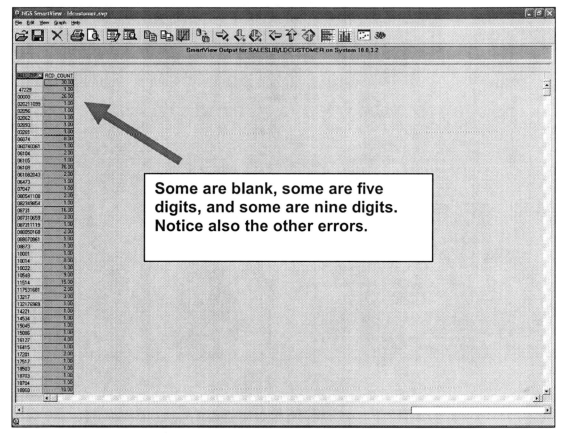

Figure 6.11

The errors shown above were found using data warehouse edits and audits run against the legacy customer master file. Customer address errors (including the zip codes) are now corrected using PERZIP4, an address cleansing software package certified by the USPS.

Many other data audits are also run. Edit or audit results are published monthly to track data correction (or lack of it).

Following is an example of customer setup edits and audits we review each month.

10/21/2005	Soft-Pak Data Audit - Calendar 2005 Combined Markets				10:38 AM

		Customer Records Audit Results	April	April	May	May
C	21	Customers with **TYPSRC blank**	127		205	
O	22	Customers with **CRES blank**	9		13	
M	23	Customers with **Invalid Tax Body** code	24		26	
B	24	Customers with **Price List blank**	10		11	
I	25	Commercial Customers with **Sales Initials blank**		Not Counted	9,802	
N	26	Customers with **Market blank**	64		0	
E	27	Customers marked **exempt from fuel surcharge**	97,002		100,455	
D	28	Customers with **business type code blank**	136		205	
	29	Customers with **blank bill cycle**	9		11	
M	30	Residential Customers with **CHG1 and missing route or day code**	6		0	
A	31	Residential Customers with **CHG2 and missing route or day code**	159		18	
R	32	Residential Customers with **CHG3 and missing route or day code**	79		8	
K	33	Residential Customers with **CHG4 and missing route or day code**	34		7	
E	34	**Inactive bill cycle customers with a blank stop date**	255,238		255,686	
T	35	**VX VY VZ bill cycle customers with a blank stop date**	1,830		1,833	
S	36	**HD, TH bill cycle customers with a blank stop date**	3,083		4,110	
	37	**Customers on any H bill cycle with a non 0 balance due**	15		16	
	38	**A1 price code customers without * as price list pos. 1**	6,902		6,978	
	39	**Res, price list * customers without 20401231 expiration date**	1,134		594	
	40	**Price list * customers with blank contract ID**	1,805		1,272	
	41	Commercial Customers with **ABCD code blank or invalid**	136		205	
	42	Commercial Customers with **ABCD code A out of range**	3,396		2,830	
	43	Commercial Customers with **ABCD code B out of range**	2,772		2,072	
	44	Commercial Customers with **ABCD code C out of range**	12,639		9,565	
	45	Commercial Customers with **ABCD code D out of range**	555		611	
	46	Customers with a **zero start date**	0		0	
	47	Customers with **service zip code** blank				

Figure 6.12

The data warehouse provides a view of data detail never before easily available!

Data Cleansing Lessons Learned

- Start data cleansing as early as possible in the project. If you don't cleanse the data, selection filters will not work properly!

BUILD – Building Data Warehouse Files

After data copy queries have been run and a staging area has been built, the next step is to build the actual files for the data warehouse. Build queries are created by the data warehouse developer. These queries create data warehouse files that will be accessed by data warehouse users and will drive the creation of data marts.

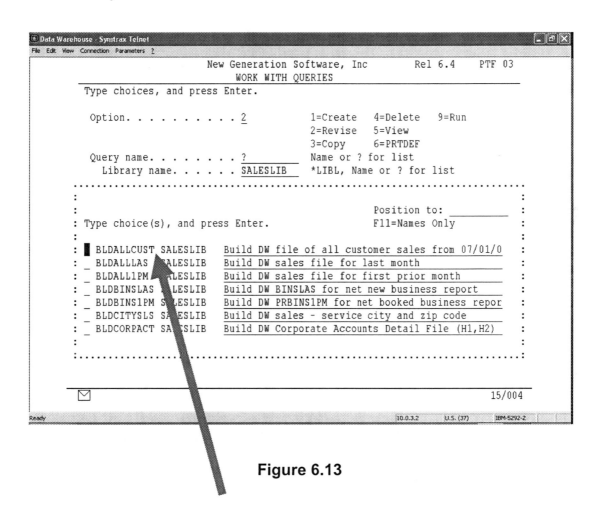

Figure 6.13

For example, the query BLDALLCUST creates a data warehouse file containing all legacy billing system sale transaction file records from July 1, 2003 forward. The output file from this query becomes the "driver" file used to create subsequent load queries as well as input to build queries for data marts. The queries listed after BLDALLCUST all create data marts. (See Step 7.) Build queries run daily, weekly, monthly, or on any predefined cycle needed by users. Each query can call a query to be run next. Nightly, weekly, or monthly data warehouse build procedures are organized to build data warehouse files first. Then, queries to build data marts are run.

LOAD - Using OLAP Engine

Load queries are created to retrieve and view data warehouse and data mart information. Load queries are made available to an OLAP engine. NGS Qport Access™ will be used to illustrate the process.

Following are a sample set of load queries.

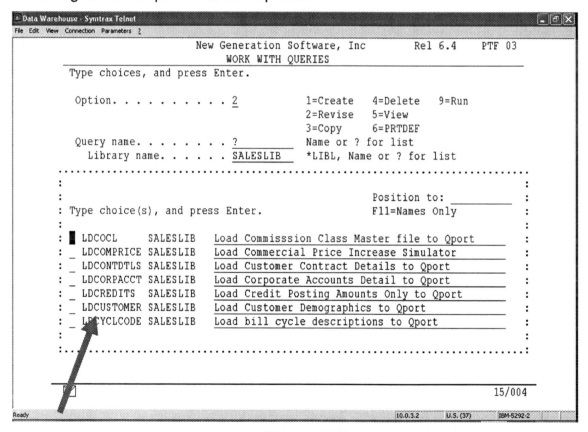

Figure 6.14

LDCUSTOMER allows OLAP access to customer demographic information placed in the data warehouse. The query also allows an OLAP user to filter information in the file by using predefined selection filters. The load process begins with launching Qport Access from a Windows user desktop with the following icon:

Figure 6.15

After Qport Access has started, the following panel will display:

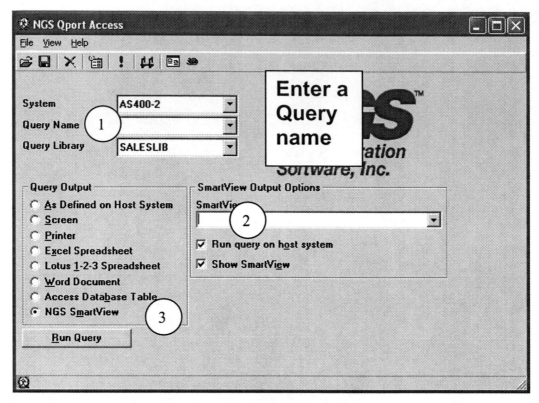

Figure 6.16

The user must then enter a query name for Qport Access to run **(1)**. If the Query Output selection is NGS SmartView **(3)**, then the query name must also be entered under SmartView Output Options **(2)**.

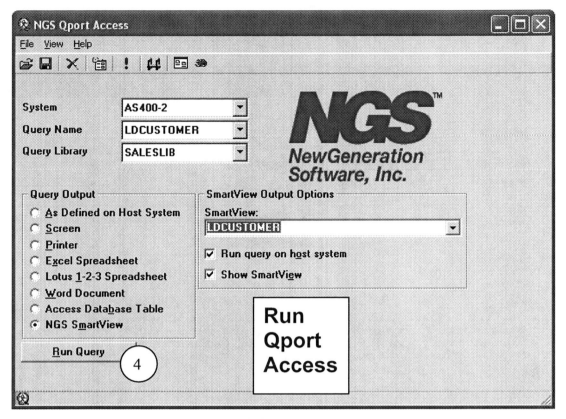

Figure 6.17

After these entries are made, the user will click on 'Run Query' **(4)**.

Panels with selection filters will display (5).

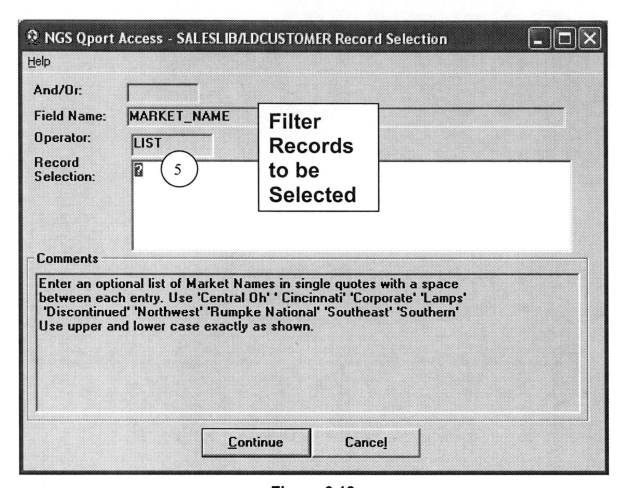

Figure 6.18

Instructions for using the filter panel are entered by the query developer and are displayed in the Comments section of the panel. For example, the above selection will filter sales records by market name.

This filter panel illustrates selecting only 'Corporate' **(6)** customers.

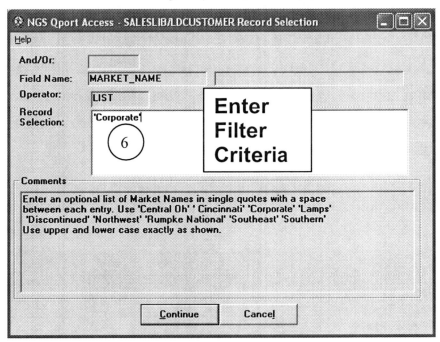

Figure 6.19

Next, we could select a specific company **(7)** assigned to the corporate accounts market.

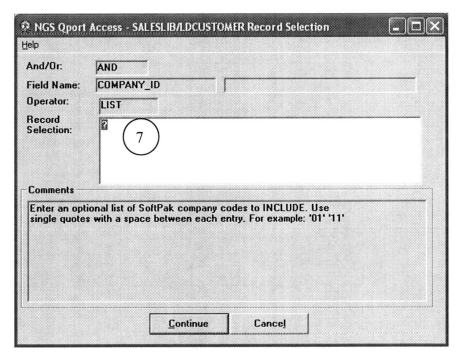

Figure 6.20

Here we could further filter records by selecting a specific company identification within the corporate market. One question mark (?) identifies an optional entry. Two question marks (??) identify a required entry. LDCUSTOMER contains 54 panels to filter customer records. Panel selections can include or exclude records. Lists can be used. Numeric ranges, including dates, can also be used. The following table is from the data warehouse user manual.

Selection panels will display in LDCUSTOMER to filter customers summarized as follows:

Select By	Required Entry?	Allowed Entry	Quotes Used?
Include by Market Name	No	One Required	Yes
Include by Soft-Pak Company	No	List	Yes
Include by Soft-Pak Customer Number	No	List	No
Include by Customer Name	No	List	Yes
Include by Customer Name	No	Like	Yes
Include Residential Customers?	No	'Y', 'N'	Yes
Include by Permanent, Temporary or both customer types	No	'P', 'T', or ' ' for both types	Yes
Include by Service Type (LOB)	No	List	Yes
Exclude by Service Type (LOB)	No	Nlist	Yes
Include by Retention Code (TYPSRC)	No	List	Yes
Exclude by Retention Code (TYPSRC)	No	Nlist	Yes
Include by Customer Start Date	No	Range	No
Include by Customer Stop Date	No	Range	No
Include by cancelled cycle flag	No	Equal	Yes
Include by first character of the Bill Cycle	No	List	Yes
Exclude by first character of the Bill Cycle	No	NList	Yes
Include by Bill Cycle	No	List	Yes
Exclude by Bill Cycle	No	NList	Yes
Include by Previous Bill Cycle	No	List	Yes
Include or Exclude customers from a fuel surcharge	No	'X' = exclude ' ' = include	Yes
Include by Price Code	No	List	Yes
Exclude by Price Code	No	NList	Yes
Include by 5 Digit Service Zip Code	No	List	Yes
Exclude by 5 Digit Service Zip Code	No	NList	Yes
Include by Tax Body Code Pos. 1	No	List	Yes
Exclude by Tax Body Code Pos. 1	No	NList	Yes
Include by Tax Body Code	No	List	Yes

Select By	Required Entry?	Allowed Entry	Quotes Used?
Exclude by Tax Body Code	No	Nlist	Yes
Include by range of Tax Body Codes	No	Range	Yes
Include by Price List Code Pos. 1	No	List	Yes
Exclude by Price List Code Pos. 1	No	NList	Yes
Include by Price List Code	No	List	Yes
Exclude by Price List Code	No	NList	Yes
Include by Sales Person by Initials	No	List	Yes
Exclude by Sales Person by Initials	No	NList	Yes
Include by Profit Center	No	List	Yes
Exclude by Profit Center	No	NList	Yes
Include by Charge Code 1	No	List	Yes
Include by Charge Code 2	No	List	Yes
Include by Charge Code 3	No	List	Yes
Include by Charge Code 4	No	List	Yes
Include by Bin Size Code (LDSERVICES only)	No	List	Yes
Exclude by Bin Size Code (LDSERVICES only)	No	NList	Yes
Include by Bin Charge Code (LDSERVICES only)	No	List	Yes
Exclude by Bin Charge Code (LDSERVICES only)	No	NList	Yes
Include by Contract Expiration date range	No	Range	No
Include by County Description	No	List	Yes
Include by Township Description	No	List	Yes
Include by ABCD Code	No	List	Yes
Exclude by ABCD Code	No	NList	Yes
Include by Monthly Billing Range (CMTH$)	No	Range	No
Include National Account #	No	Equal	Yes
Include route 1 (LDCUSTOMER only)	No	List	Yes
Include route 2 (LDCUSTOMER only)	No	List	Yes
Include route 3 (LDCUSTOMER only)	No	List	Yes
Include route 4 (LDCUSTOMER only)	No	List	Yes
Include by Special Charge Operator (LDSERVICES only)	No	List	Yes

Figure 6.21

Load Lessons Learned

- Bring the lowest level of data your application system supports into the data warehouse. If you do not do it at the beginning of the project, you will probably have to do it later!

- Don't ever write an OLAP process with 54 panels of filters! Keep load selection functions as simple as possible.

A Quick Review

Constructing the data warehouse can be viewed in a few easy steps – but that doesn't mean it's not a lot of work! Here are the steps:

- Copy the desired data to a staging area.
- Cleanse the data.
- Build a set of data warehouse dimensional and flat files using meta data.
- Construct a set of load queries or programs to be used to access and filter data.

Remember Kanter's law from the beginning of this section of the methodology. Almost everything can look like a failure while you're in the middle of it! My experience has been that if you persevere, both you and your company will realize tremendous benefit.

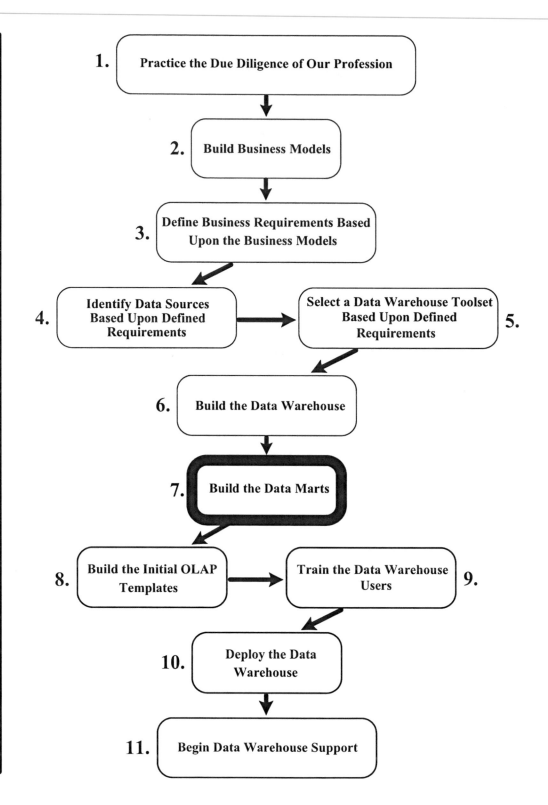

<< Data Warehouse Implementation Methodology Steps >>

1. Practice the Due Diligence of Our Profession

2. Build Business Models

3. Define Business Requirements Based Upon the Business Models

4. Identify Data Sources Based Upon Defined Requirements

5. Select a Data Warehouse Toolset Based Upon Defined Requirements

6. Build the Data Warehouse

7. Build the Data Marts

8. Build the Initial OLAP Templates

9. Train the Data Warehouse Users

10. Deploy the Data Warehouse

11. Begin Data Warehouse Support

> **"Don't stand shivering upon the bank;
> plunge in at once, and have it over."**
> *Sam Slick*

Step 7: Build the Data Marts

A data mart presents a subset of data warehouse information and is used to segregate information by certain predefined criteria. For example, the sales data warehouse contains one record for every sale from July 1, 2003 forward – over 13,000,000 records. However, we have a number of reports only needing sales for the current month. The sales data mart for last month contains about 700,000 records – 12,300,000 fewer records to pass!

In Step 7, we will build three data marts for sales:

- BLDALLCUST – current month sales
- BLDALLLAS – last month's sales
- BLDALL1PM – penultimate (next to last) month sales

The data warehouse month end process copies and builds files for the data warehouse.

121

BLDALLCUST – Current Month Sales

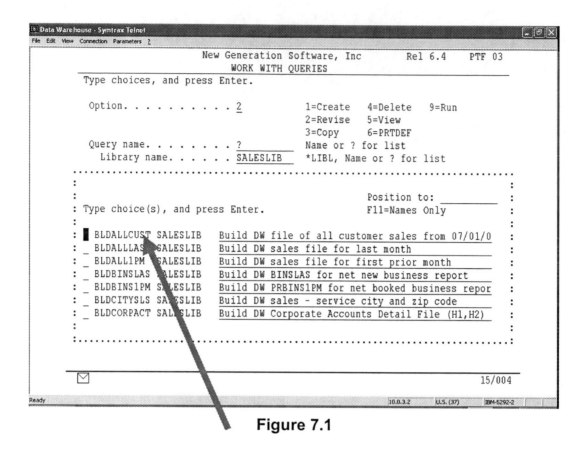

Figure 7.1

Each month end, query BLDALLCUST builds a new data warehouse file, adding the new month's sales records. We keep two prior years plus the current year's sales in the data warehouse.

Following is the SELECT RECORDS panel for data warehouse query BLDALLCUST.

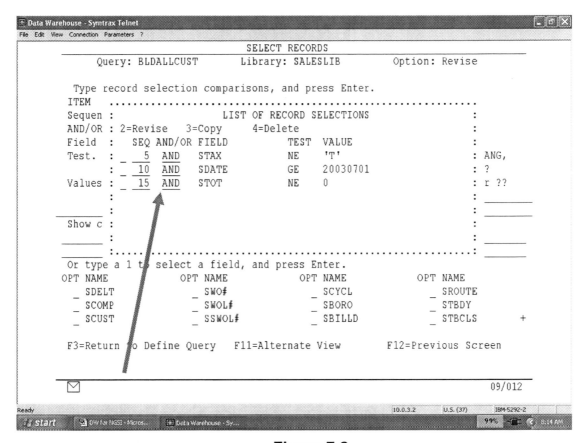

Figure 7.2

Sale file records with a non-zero sale total, a sales tax identifier not equal to 'T' (not a "tax" charge), and a sale date greater or equal to July 1, 2003, are moved to the data warehouse.

A control file has been developed to identify queries for the month and year of the last month, as well as the penultimate month for data warehouse and data mart build. The control file is updated (using WRKDFU) each month as the step before running any data warehouse month-end build queries. This method is not very elegant but is workable. Feel free to find a better way to do this.

A couple of fields were added for future use when the control file was created. Field YRMTHFUT1 is used to give the data warehouse copy queries a starting month and year for all records brought to the data warehouse. Field YRMTHFUT2 is provided just in case there is another query need. The control file format is shown below.

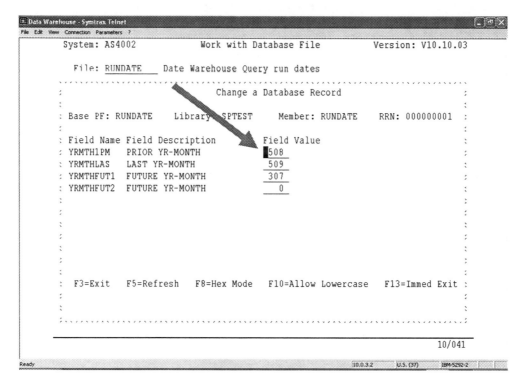

Figure 7.3

BLDALLLAS – Last Month Sales

Query BLDALLLAS creates a data mart for last month's sales. This query uses the field YRMTHLAS from the control file.

Below is the SELECT RECORDS panel for data mart query BLDALLLAS.

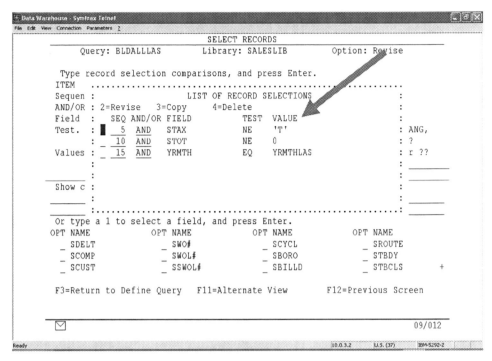

Figure 7.4

BLDALL1PM – Penultimate Month Sales

Query BLDALL1PM uses the same control file to build the penultimate month data mart. This query uses control file field YRMTH1PM.

Just as there are three month's views for the sales file, so are there for the current services file and customer file.

For example, LDSERVICE is the load query for the current services file (called BINS). Three queries rebuild copies of the data warehouse file containing services (used by LDSERVICE) provided to customers:

- BLDBINSCUR builds the current month BINS file.
- BLDBINSLAS builds last month's BINS file.
- BLDBINS1PM builds the penultimate BINS file.

These sets of files are used to create a Net New Business report and a Net Booked Business report using information from the data warehouse and data marts. These reports are new to the company and were not available in our operations software package.

Following is an example of the Net New Business Report.

Market Segment	A Total Sales For January, 2005 [1]		B Feb-05 New Customer $ [2]		C NET $ change to existing Customers [3]		D February Lost Permanent Customer $ [4]		E Net New Sales $ as of COB February 2005 [5]	F February Net Business Change [6]	G Total Sales For February 2005 [7]	G - A [8]
Central Oh	4,118,740.62	+	142,238.04	+	92,869.45	-	6,156.77	=	4,347,691.34	228,950.72	4,474,673.08	355,932.46
Cincinnati	10,155,772.60	+	15,211.36	+	(16,372.38)	-	(3,905.15)	=	10,158,516.73	2,744.13	10,768,880.46	613,107.86
Corporate	417,371.25	+	255.79	+	(7,080.69)	-	(69.28)	=	410,615.63	(6,755.62)	503,065.71	85,694.46
Discontinued	603.11	+	0.00	+	(14.67)	-	0.00	=	588.44	(14.67)	1,154.78	551.67
Lamps	29,620.83	+	0.00	+	(4,486.68)	-	0.00	=	25,134.15	(4,486.68)	(56.00)	(29,676.83)
Northwest	2,168,886.47	+	3,509.94	+	51,594.45	-	1,089.10	=	2,222,901.76	54,015.29	2,650,770.21	481,883.74
Southeast	4,269,893.17	+	10,527.63	+	125,719.85	-	4,513.40	=	4,401,627.25	131,734.08	3,765,654.78	(504,238.39)
Southern	2,511,675.37	+	37,145.30	+	(14,656.12)	-	16,931.29	=	2,517,233.26	5,557.89	2,639,006.60	127,331.23
Unknown	0.00	+	0.00	+	0.00	-	0.00	=	0.00	0.00	0.00	0.00
Totals->	23,672,563.42	+	208,888.06	+	227,573.21	-	24,716.13	=	24,084,308.56	411,745.14	24,803,149.62	411,745.14

Column Notes	
(1)	Total dollar amount of business shown as active in the SoftPak SALE file after COB 2/28/05 (LDALL1PM [11])
(2)	Sales for customers with a start date in January, 2005 (LDNEWCUST [11])
(3)	Change in billing amounts for existing customers with billings in January and February 2005 (LDCHNGCUST [11])
(4)	Billing amounts for permenant customers with a stop date in February 2005 and a billing cycle starting with 'X' (LDLOSTCUST [11])
(5)	Net new business calculated as columns: ((A + B + C) - D).
(6)	Net business change calculated as column: (E - A).
(7)	Total dollar amount of business shown as active in the SoftPak SALE file after COB 2/28/05 (LDALLLAS [11])
(8)	February 2005 sales minus January 2005 sales
(11)	Data Warehouse query used to extract data from SoftPack SALE file

Figure 7.5

Using the above method, once BLDALLCUST has run to add a new month to the data warehouse, *any* data mart build needing a set of updated data warehouse sale file data can be run.

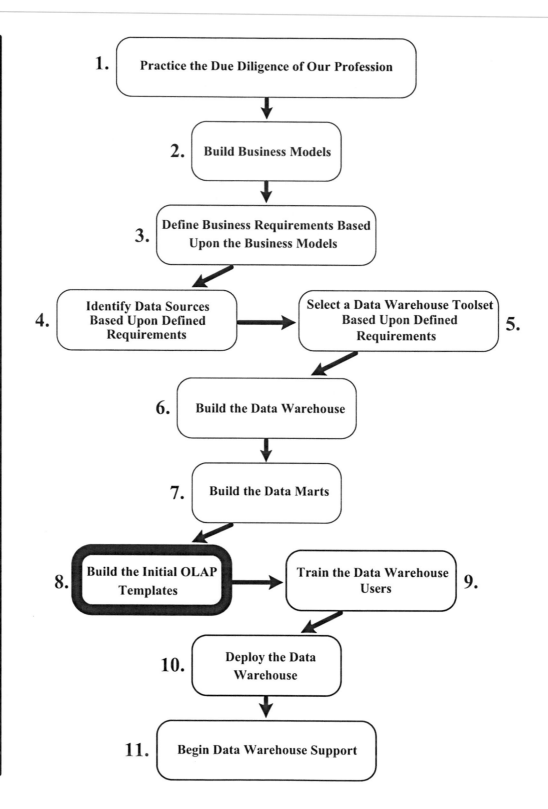

<< Data Warehouse Implementation Methodology Steps >>

1. Practice the Due Diligence of Our Profession

2. Build Business Models

3. Define Business Requirements Based Upon the Business Models

4. Identify Data Sources Based Upon Defined Requirements

5. Select a Data Warehouse Toolset Based Upon Defined Requirements

6. Build the Data Warehouse

7. Build the Data Marts

8. Build the Initial OLAP Templates

9. Train the Data Warehouse Users

10. Deploy the Data Warehouse

11. Begin Data Warehouse Support

> **"One must learn by doing the thing;**
> **for though you think you know it,**
> **you have no certainty until you try."**
> *Sophocles*

Step 8:   Build the Initial OLAP Templates

Our data warehouse deployment tactics did not (and still do not) include giving the user community the ability to construct its own copy, build or load queries. We provided an initial set of load queries employing standard measurement metrics and standard record filter criteria. This tactic established consensus during MOR (monthly operations review) meetings. Consensus was also established at the line management level within the company.

The initial goals of these initial templates were to:

- Provide access to customer demographics.
- Identify service to be provided to customers.
- Perform sales analysis.
- Make available one company-wide source for business intelligence.

Initial copy and build queries were developed to support those goals. Our first three load queries were LDCUSTOMER, LDSERVICES, and LDSALES. These queries answered the questions:

- Who are our customers?
- What services do we provide our customers?
- What is the sales volume of these services to our customers?

These load templates are the most straightforward queries that will be created. Review Appendix F (LDSALES) to understand a load query.

Load queries must all have the same look and feel. The goal is that once a customer understands how to use one load query, he or she will understand how to use them all! The following LDSALES panels represent the general look and feel of the load queries. They were created using NGS' Qport Access™.

Respond to record selection filters...

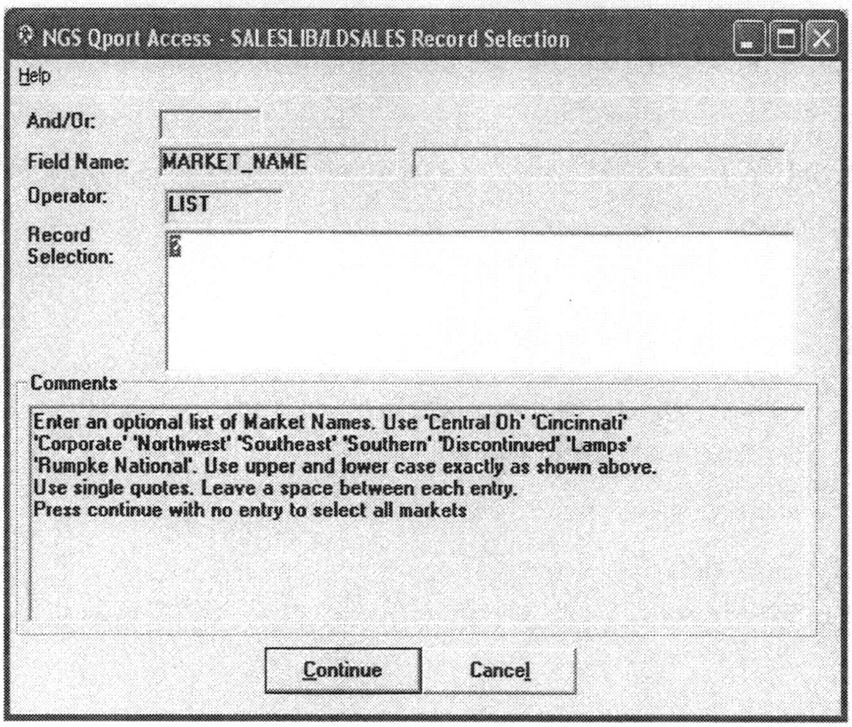

Figure 8.1

LDSALES contains 23 selection filter panels. The user will click Continue until all record selection panels are displayed and desired entries are made. The OLAP engine will then select the desired records – depending on the correctness of the selection entries, of course!

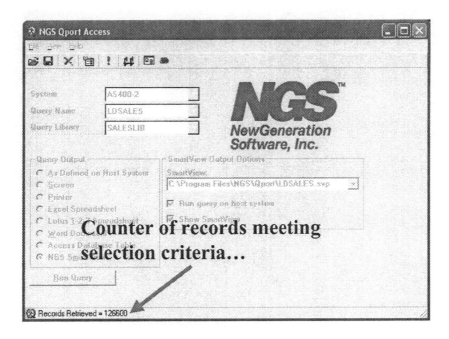

Figure 8.2

A counter of selected records will display, followed by a Data File Fields selection panel (in this example, the three-dimensional view).

OLAP data field selection panel...

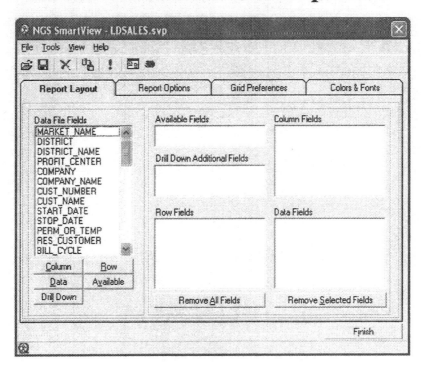

Figure 8.3

The OLAP user will drag and drop fields to desired locations in the panel.

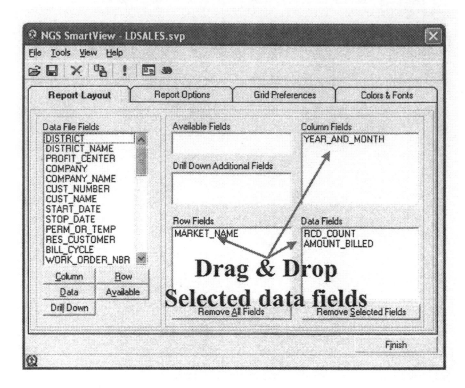

Figure 8.4

When fields have been placed, the user will click Finish to display the results.

Then, the OLAP three-dimensional view panel will display.

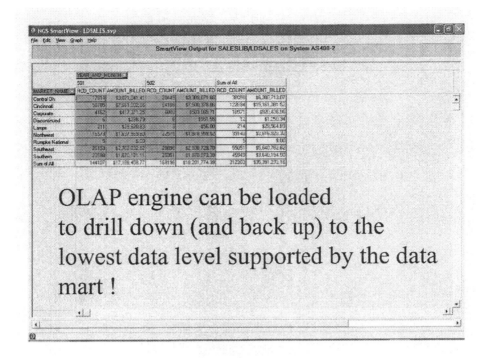

Figure 8.5

Finally, a graph, if desired, can easily be prepared.

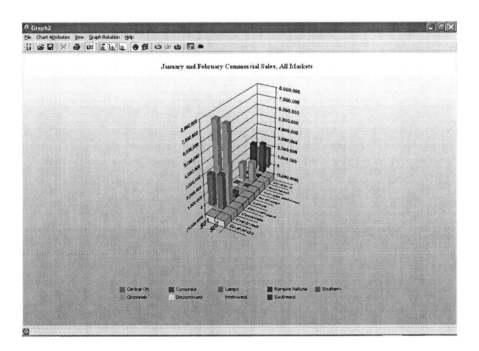

Figure 8.6

Lessons Learned

- If you plan to output from an OLAP engine to EXCEL, use one line column headings. Otherwise, EXCEL power users will complain because EXCEL pivot tables can only deal with one row of headings!
- The concept of two-dimensional data views is easy to teach. The concept of three-dimensional views is much more difficult to teach!

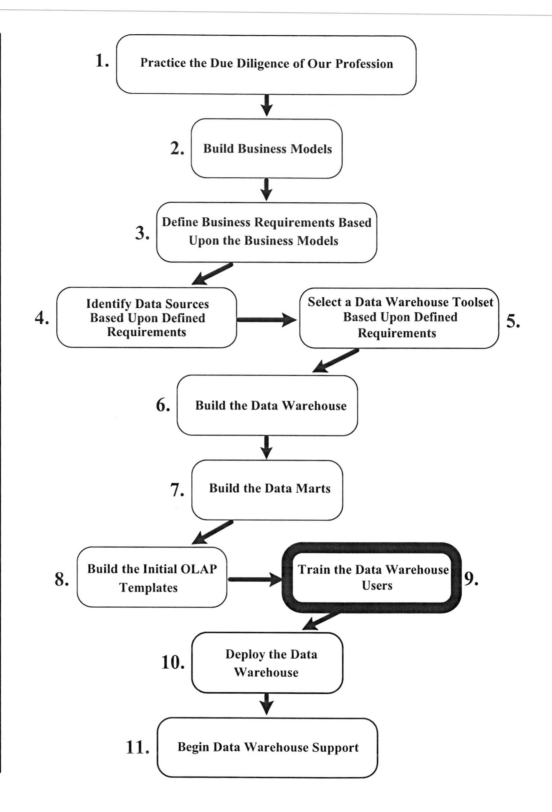

<< Data Warehouse Implementation Methodology Steps >>

1. Practice the Due Diligence of Our Profession

2. Build Business Models

3. Define Business Requirements Based Upon the Business Models

4. Identify Data Sources Based Upon Defined Requirements

5. Select a Data Warehouse Toolset Based Upon Defined Requirements

6. Build the Data Warehouse

7. Build the Data Marts

8. Build the Initial OLAP Templates

9. Train the Data Warehouse Users

10. Deploy the Data Warehouse

11. Begin Data Warehouse Support

> **"Education is the most powerful weapon we can use to change the world."**
> *Nelson Mandella*

Step 9:   Train the Data Warehouse Users

Phases of Adult Learning

Bill Miller, President of Performance Leadership, LLC, identified two phases of adult training. The following diagram depicts those phases:

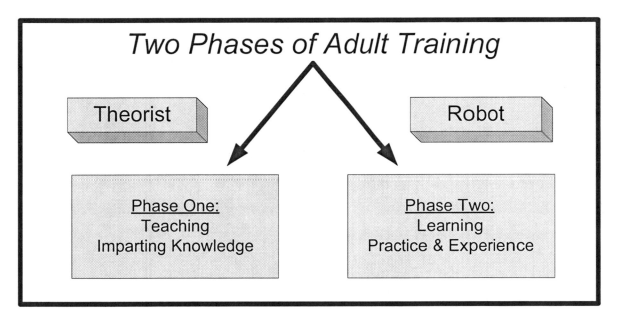

Figure 9.1

Adult training programs should provide two types of training: teaching and educating to impart knowledge, and practicing to learn and build skills. When we overemphasize teaching and imparting knowledge, we produce "theorists" who have a lot of ideas. They know the "what's" and the "why's" of the job, but they lack the skills to do it.

Conversely, overemphasis on skill building without knowledge produces "robots." Robots are people going through the motions of the job. They are running around "doing the rules." But since they lack knowledge, they lose creativity and their full human potential. And when something occurs outside of the rules, they are completely lost.

Miller further identified five steps within the two phases of adult training:

- Tell them what to do
- Show them what to do
- Let them try
- Observe performance
- Respond with praise or redirect

Malcom Knowles – The Father of Adult Learning Theory

In his 1988 book *The Modern Practice of Adult Education: from pedagogy to andragogy*, Malcolm Knowles suggested a comprehensive adult learning theory. For Knowles, adult learning was process based rather than content based. He suggested five main assumptions about the characteristics of adult learners that make them different from child learners:

- *Self-concept:* as people mature, they move toward being self directed.
- *Experience:* as people mature, they accumulate life experiences. And those life experiences become a reservoir that provides an increasing resource for learning.
- *Readiness to learn:* as people mature, readiness to learn becomes increasingly oriented to development tasks required by their social roles.
- *Orientation to learning:* as people mature, their perspective changes to immediate application of knowledge.
- *Motivation to learn:* as people mature, the motivation to learn becomes internal.

Jane Vella – Founder of Global Learning Partners, Inc.

Jane Villa identifies twelve principles for adult learning in her book *Learning to Listen, Learning to Teach: The Power of Dialogue in Educating Adults*:

- Needs assessment – participation of the learners in naming what is to be learned.
- Safety in the environment and the process. We can create a context for learning. And that context can be made safe.
- Sound relationships between teacher and learner and among learners.
- Sequence of content and reinforcement.
- Praxis – action with three flexion or learning by doing.
- Respect for learners as decision makers.
- Ideas, feelings, and actions – cognitive, affective, and psychomotor aspects of learning.
- Immediacy of the learning.
- Clear roles and role development.
- Teamwork in the use of small groups.
- Engagement of the learners in what they're learning.
- Accountability – how do they know that they know?

A Message to Instructors

And finally, here is a message to instructors from Stephen Lieb, senior technical writer and planner at Arizona Department of Health Services and part-time instructor with Southern Mountain Community College:

> "Part of being an effective instructor involves understanding how adults learn best. Compared to children and teens, adults have special needs and requirements as learners. Despite the apparent truth, adult learning is a relatively new area of study. The adult field of learning was pioneered by

Malcolm Knowles. He identified the following characteristics of adult learners:

Adults are autonomous and self directed. They need to be free to direct themselves. Their teachers must actively involve adult participants in the learning process and serve as facilitators for them. Specifically, they must get participants' perspectives about what topics to cover and let them work on projects that reflect their interests. They should allow the participants to assume responsibility for presentations and group leadership. They have to be sure to act as facilitators, guiding participants to their own knowledge rather than supplying them with facts. Finally, they must show participants how the class will help them reach their goals.

Adults have accumulated a foundation of life experiences and knowledge that may include work related activities, family responsibilities, and previous education they need to connect to learning to this knowledge/experience base. To help them do so, instructors should draw out participants' experience and knowledge which is relevant to the topic. They must relate theories and concepts to the participants and recognize the value of experience in learning.

Adults are goal oriented. Upon enrolling in a course, they usually know what goal they want to attain. They, therefore, appreciate an educational program that is organized and has clearly defined elements. Instructors must show participants how this class will help them obtain their goals. This classification of goals and course objectives must be done early in the course.

Adults are relevancy oriented. They must see a reason for learning something. Learning has to be applicable to their work or other responsibilities to be of value to them. Therefore, instructors must identify objectives for adult participants before the course begins. This means, also, that theories and concepts must be related to a setting familiar to participants. This need can be fulfilled by letting participants choose projects that reflect their own interests.

Adults are practical, focusing on the aspects of a lesson most useful to them in their work. They may not be interested in knowledge for its own sake. Instructors must tell participants explicitly how the lesson will be useful to them on the job.

As do all learners, adults need to be shown respect. Instructors must acknowledge the wealth of experience that adult participants bring to the classroom. These adults should be treated as equals in experience and knowledge and allowed to voice their opinions freely in class."

Appendix J contains another useful perspective on training adults: "30 Things We Know for Sure About Adult Learning," by Ron and Susan Zemke (ProQuest Educational Journals, 1988).

Understanding of all this material – the phases of adult learning as diagramed by Bill Miller, Malcolm Knowles' adult learning theory, the adult learning principles described by Jane Vella, Steven Lieb's perspective on the work of Malcolm Knowles, and the Zemkes' perspective on training adults – will provide an excellent grounding on how to teach adults as you prepare the materials to train users of the data warehouse.

Data Warehouse User Documentation

The data warehouse is not a success unless it is being used.

Good training is the most important step toward successful use. Development of a user manual is the beginning of successful training. The user manual needs to be both a reference manual and a user guide.

- The reference manual section describes *what the data warehouse is.*
- The user manual section describes *how to use it.*
- The reference manual section answers the question: *What can I do* with the data warehouse?
- The user guide section answers the question: *How do I do it* with the data warehouse?

The user manual can be the document used for training. Our user manual begins with a short overview of data warehousing. The overview section ends with a diagram depicting a data warehouse model specific to my company. The next section is a very detailed set of instructions for using the sales reporting capability of the data warehouse. This detailed section is used for training. The following sections describe specific data warehouse functions. The last section contains technical and process documentation. Users want to know, for instance, how often the data warehouse is updated. This section also lists the copy and build record selection criteria.

After the user manual has been written, user training must begin.

An Outline for User Documentation

Following is the general (but not complete – a number of data marts are not shown) outline of the document provided to data warehouse users at my company. The document is also used for training. In its current form, it is approximately 150 pages. Appendix G contains the complete table of contents.

Section 1

- Data warehouse overview
- Data warehouse terminology
- Data warehouse components
- Data warehouse startup methodology
- Our company data warehouse model

Section 2

- Sales reporting data mart
- Data elements available in the sales data mart
- Sales data mart example – loading roll-off data into Qport Access
- Preparing net new business information
- Preparing net lost business information
- Analyzing customer set up in demographics
- Data elements available in the customer data mart
- Customer record selection
- Vehicle unit cost data mart
- Data elements available in the vehicle data mart
- Vehicle record selection
- Fixed asset data mart
- Data elements available in the fixed asset data mart
- Asset record selection
- Summary of record selection by data mart
- Determining productivity and profitability

- Determining truck cost and utilization

Section 3

- Preparing the data warehouse each day
- Preparing the data warehouse each week
- Preparing the data warehouse each month
- Updated information immediately available in the data warehouse

Section 1 of the document is the user manual. This section describes what a data warehouse is and how it is implemented at our company.

Section 2 begins with a very detailed set of instructions on how to use the sales data mart. Because the OLAP engine works the same way regardless of the data mart, subsequent data mart instructions can be less detailed. The user manual ends with a summary of record selection filters for each data mart and discussion of using the data mart to establish productivity, profitability, truck cost, and utilization. These discussions provide common ground for all markets and operational units within the company to arrive at consensus during the MOR (monthly operations review) process. The operating groups now have one version of the truth available for reporting, whether it is in the boardroom or in the shop.

Section 3 identifies when information is available in the data warehouse. Remember that we had been requested to move from monthly, to weekly, to daily, to immediate access.

Appendix L contains a sample of Section 3 of our data warehouse user manual.

Restating the Importance of Training
for Data Warehousing Success

Success with a data warehouse project is measured by use, not by elegant application of technology. You may be able to identify a pressing need within the company and then architect an innovative data warehouse solution to meet that need, but if the staff that the solution is designed for cannot be efficiently and effectively trained to use the data warehouse, you have failed. Not only have you failed, but the concept of implementing a data warehouse within your company has also failed. The benefits of successful data warehouse implementation are very high; but the damage from failure can also be very high.

Lessons Learned

- The user manual should be available online. Our experience is that the document is continually changing and growing. Don't try to keep printed copies updated.
- Do short training sessions but repeat them – train often, until the users are comfortable with the data warehouse.
- The concept of two-dimensional data views is very easy to teach. The concept of three-dimensional data views is much harder to teach.
- Exploit the vendors' knowledge of their product.
- Keep training expense in the business case for the project – or don't do the project!
- It is not enough to teach data warehouse users how to use the toolset. You also have to teach them how to use the information!
- Be VERY, VERY patient....

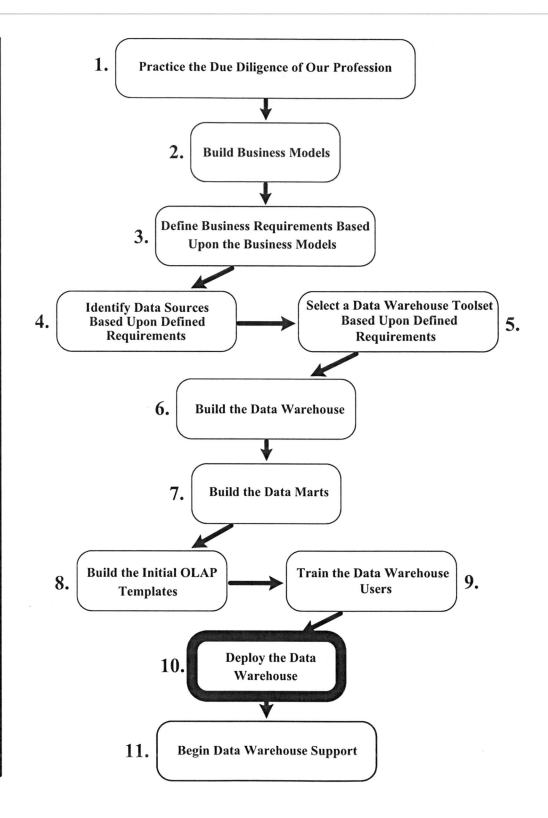

<< Data Warehouse Implementation Methodology Steps >>

1. Practice the Due Diligence of Our Profession

2. Build Business Models

3. Define Business Requirements Based Upon the Business Models

4. Identify Data Sources Based Upon Defined Requirements

5. Select a Data Warehouse Toolset Based Upon Defined Requirements

6. Build the Data Warehouse

7. Build the Data Marts

8. Build the Initial OLAP Templates

9. Train the Data Warehouse Users

10. Deploy the Data Warehouse

11. Begin Data Warehouse Support

> **"Behold the Turtle. He never makes progress
> until he sticks his neck out."**
> *Anonymous*

Step 10: <u>Deploy the Data Warehouse</u>

Deployment, according to Dr. Kimball, is "the convergence of technology, data, and applications on the business user's desks, along with the necessary education and user support structure."

That convergence of technology, data, and applications is the topic of Step 10.

The deployment strategy at our company has been to release one category of data warehouse function at a time. The category deployed first provided sales analysis (LDSALES). We created the initial OLAP templates to facilitate training the sales group in the use of the data warehouse and to insure that their needs were being meet. We wanted an early and visible victory (sales people talk a lot) to highlight the data warehouse possibilities within the company. A "beat the bully" strategy allowed us to solve the sales group's most urgent needs first. The most urgent need at that time was correctly determining "net new business" and "net booked business" each month. The next most urgent need was reconciling sales group reported sales to the general ledger. After those initial successes, we started receiving "By the way, I really would like to…." phone calls.

Use of the data warehouse gathered momentum as the possibilities of it became evident to the company. Another early success with the sales group was giving them the ability to do sales analysis using filtering information from the sales transaction file. That analysis empowered them to view product sales and costs within each line of business detailing markets, districts, companies, salesperson, product types, and about a dozen additional filter criteria. They were finally able to analyze sales the way they were required to budget sales.

There are a number of deployment issues that need to be addressed, hopefully, before deployment:

- Determining user software and hardware configuration requirements
- Determining adequacy of bandwidth across the data transport infrastructure
- Establishing grouping and security architecture

Determining User Software and Hardware Configuration Requirements

Our initial expectation of departmental use of the data warehouse was shortsighted. Once discussion of user information availability began to move through our organization, we began to receive more and more requests for access to the data warehouse. Unfortunately, we had not done a thorough study of laptop and desktop devices used throughout the company. For example, we now deploy the data warehouse to users with Windows-based terminals running on CITRIX. We had made no provision within our toolset to support CITRIX users. Additionally, we underestimated the amount of memory required on laptops and desktop PCs. Data warehouse users now all have 1GB of RAM. What's the lesson? Think beyond your initial expectation and prepare early for success.

Determining Infrastructure Adequacy

Our infrastructure now supports T1 speeds between locations. Review your infrastructure bandwidth early and be prepared to increase it if needed. Again, we were not totally prepared for the success of this project.

Establishing Security Architecture

In the functional requirements we defined in Step 5 of the methodology, we listed a number of security requirements:

- The ability to operate in complete accordance with i5/OS security standards at all levels.
- The ability to have file/data accessibility based on standard operating system security.
- The ability to secure data access at the file, record, and field levels by user profile.
- The ability to secure queries so only authorized users can modify and run them.
- The ability to secure queries so only authorized users can distribute output as an attachment to an e-mail message.
- The ability to secure queries so only authorized users can distribute output into Office 2003 productivity tools.

Even though much of the data warehouse was not live production data, a high level of security was required.

We built the data warehouse to make it possible for less technical business users to pull out the most meaningful things about business performance, for example:

- Where are we making or losing money?
- Who are our most and least profitable customers?
- What products are selling well?
- Are we productive?
- Are we profitable?

We wanted business intelligence available, but we wanted it under the umbrella of a robust security system. We wanted a toolset that would use all of the power of i5/OS but that would also give us complete security at the record and field level. We wanted security control of our data warehouse at four levels: library, file, record, and field levels. We also wanted control of data warehouse queries at the query library, query, and query option level. For example, we wanted to restrict a user to queries in a special library setup for his department and we wanted to restrict that user to viewing and running only certain queries within that library. We also wanted to organize security around users within workgroups. That workgroup strategy worked well for us. We have workgroups now organized around specific tasks such as sales, truck maintenance, operations, financial analysis, the senior administration and others. A business analyst within the Information Technology department has responsibility for making security changes, and changes are only made through the work request process. That means that changes must be approved by management.

Lessons Learned

- Work with the management team at all levels in the company during deployment. Use of the data warehouse must be managed. Some of our senior managers complain that their staff is now spending too much time analyzing information and not enough time effecting change!
- Absolutely do not deploy the data warehouse to anyone who has not been through toolset training.
- Investigate each device attached to the network supporting the data warehouse. We forgot about our CITRIX users!
- Thoroughly understand the memory requirements and constraints of the toolset. We hit an unanticipated 2GB boundary.

The Progression the Author Didn't Anticipate...

The initial focus of the data warehouse was to support monthly operations reviews (MORs). The data warehouse initially provided detailed sales reporting, detailed truck maintenance cost, and productivity and profitability analysis down to one truck doing one service on one day.

As the value of the data warehouse became more and more apparent and the possibilities of providing meaningful information began to be realized, we started getting requests to update certain files and tables in the data warehouse on a weekly basis. The first weekly request was to update changed customer master information to the data warehouse. Not long after that, an enterprising employee in operations dispatch requested that work order information for the following day be updated to the data warehouse each night. The updated work order information was to be used to assist with routing trucks each morning. And then finally, the sales department complained that they were not able to immediately see customer master file changes reflected in the data warehouse loads they ran.

We had begun using the data warehouse as a tool to improve the integrity of master file as well as transaction information in the operations systems, and customers wanted to see their changes reflected in the data warehouse immediately. We had moved from a monthly (after the fact reporting and analysis) to an active data warehouse. This was the progression we didn't anticipate. In the course of one year, we had moved from monthly to weekly to nightly to real time tactical capability (called an "active data warehouse" by the data warehouse and business intelligence industry) within the data warehouse.

Data warehouse access continues to grow. As of this writing, we are on a pace of over 12,000 data warehouse accesses per year; perhaps a sad commentary on the reporting and analytical capability of our legacy systems.

Lessons Learned

- Expand your view of what the data warehouse and associated business intelligence can provide your business. Identify analytics across all periods of time relevant to business operations whether it is multi-year, annual, quarterly, monthly, weekly, daily, or real time.

- Expand your vision; expect and prepare for a high level of success!

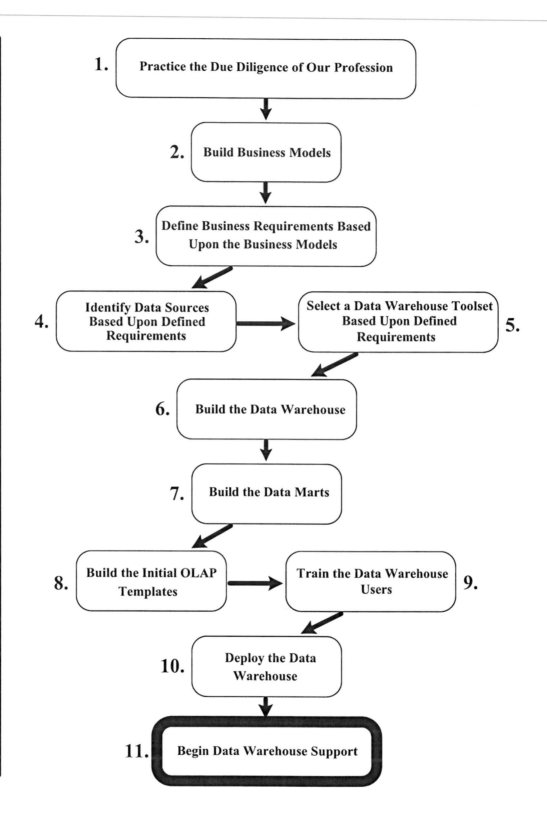

<< Data Warehouse Implementation Methodology Steps >>

1. Practice the Due Diligence of Our Profession

2. Build Business Models

3. Define Business Requirements Based Upon the Business Models

4. Identify Data Sources Based Upon Defined Requirements

5. Select a Data Warehouse Toolset Based Upon Defined Requirements

6. Build the Data Warehouse

7. Build the Data Marts

8. Build the Initial OLAP Templates

9. Train the Data Warehouse Users

10. Deploy the Data Warehouse

11. Begin Data Warehouse Support

> **"Talk doesn't cook rice."**
> *Chinese Proverb*

Step 11: <u>Begin Data Warehouse Support</u>

The data warehouse project will live or die with your level of support.

You are now a software vendor. You will be expected to provide the same level of support that is demanded from any vendor supplying software!

Lessons Learned

- Be proactive with support. If you know a department's biggest problem and can solve it for them using the data warehouse – do it! Remember, people will be talking about the data warehouse. Make the conversations positive.

- Publish how support will be provided and then actually *provide it that way!*

- Take support to the field.

- Don't wait for the user community to ask for support. They probably won't. It is easier for them to not use the data warehouse then it will be for them to ask for help. (And not using it will be your fault, because the customer is never wrong.)

- Personally give each data warehouse customer your work phone number and encourage them to use it! And if they don't call you, you call them to see how they are doing with the data warehouse.

- Don't just talk about success. Track and publish data warehouse usage!

Develop Measures of Success

Remember - the only real measure of success for a data warehouse is if it is being used!

Develop questions to measure success. For example:

Methodology Step 1:

- Do we have a defined SDLC process?
- Can our infrastructure support a data warehouse?
- Have we developed a Statement of Work?
- Have we written an RFP?
- Do we have a project sponsor?
- Do we have a realistic project budget?
- Do we have a project manager?
- Do we have a project plan?

Methodology Step 2:

- Have we developed the right models to understand the business?

Methodology Step 3:

- Have we documented needed measurement metrics?
- Do we know all KPIs and CFSs? For every level of management?
- Have we documented needed functional requirements?

Methodology Step 4:

- Have we identified needed extant data?
- Have we identified needed derived data?

156

Methodology Step 5:

- Did we get executive buy-in for our RFP?

- Do we have an effective way to compare toolsets?

- Do we really understand how to build a data warehouse with our toolset?

Methodology Steps 6 and 7:

- Do we understand what data we will copy (extract) to a data staging area?

- Do we understand which data needs cleansing and how to cleanse it?

- Do we understand which data we will build (transform) for the data warehouse?

- Do we understand what data will be moved to data marts?

Methodology Step 8:

- Do we understand what information will be made available to users through initial OLAP loads?

- Do we understand what data filters are needed?

Methodology Step 9:

- Do we understand how adults learn?

- Do we have an effective training strategy and accompanying user manual?

Methodology Step 10:

- Do we know which users will have access to the data warehouse?

- Do those users have the right equipment?

- Do we know what security will be in place?

Methodology Step 11:

- Have we documented and published a support strategy?

- Have we tracked and published data warehouse usage?

The January 2006 issue of DM Review (page 24) contains an article titled "Benchmarks for BI and Data Warehousing Success." It is an excellent article dividing 29 success metrics into four areas: information quality, system quality, individual impacts, and organizational impacts. A copy of the article can be found at DMReview.com.

Appendices

Appendix A. Two-Tier Data Warehouse Model

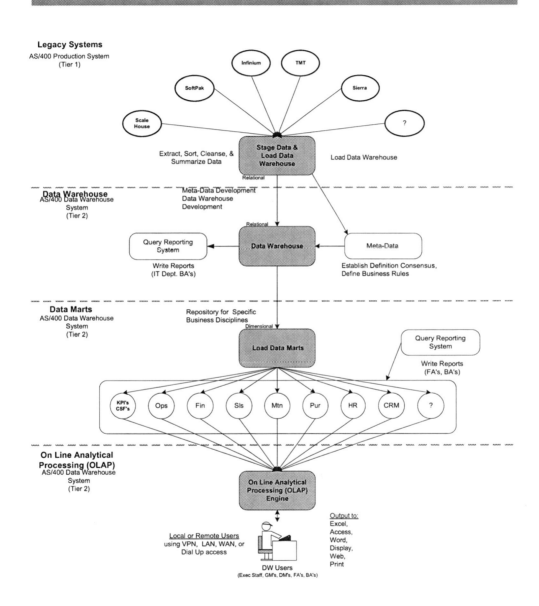

Source: New Generation Software, Inc.

Appendix B. An SDLC Methodology Diagram

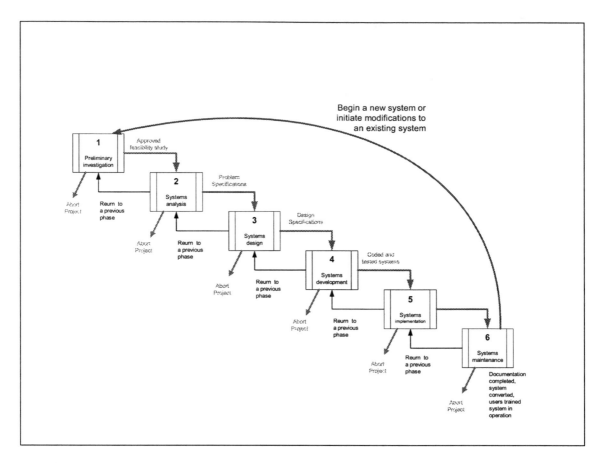

Source: Hutchinson and Sawyer (2003)

Appendix C. RFP Document Table of Contents

1. Introduction
2. Background
3. Corporate Objectives
4. Customer Profile
5. Corporate Structure
6. Technology Profile
7. Hardware Environment
8. Software Environment
9. Communications Environment
10. Business Requirements Overview
11. Process Requirements
12. Data Requirements
13. Technology Requirements
14. Current Situation Assessment
15. Vendor Response Instructions
16. Nature of RFP Process
17. Proposal Submission
18. ED TEL Responsibility
19. RFP Clarifications and Inquires
20. Evaluation Process
21. Contract Negotiation and Award
22. Vendor Contact Instructions
23. Corporate Contract
24. Closing Date
25. Format Instructions
26. Statement of Confidentiality
27. Vendor Response Format
28. Vendor Cover Sheet
29. Response Format

30. Business Requirements Evaluation Criteria

31. General Requirements

32. Process Requirements

33. Data Requirements

34. Audit and Control Requirements

35. Interfacing Requirements

36. Technology Requirements Evaluation Criteria

37. Technology Architecture

38. Application Architecture

39. Communications Architecture

40. Documentation Format

41. Capacity, Volumetric and Operational Performance

42. Operating Environment Considerations

43. Vendor Consultant Evaluation Criteria

44. Vendor Package Evaluation Criteria

45. Vendor Services Evaluation Criteria

46. Statement of Vendor Responsibility

47. Vendor Profile

48. Vendor Project Management Approach

49. Vendor Human Resources Profile

50. Appendices

Source: Kachur (2000)

Appendix D. P^2M^2 Methodology

The P^2M^2 methodology recognizes that the world is dynamic and ever changing. P^2M^2 is designed to facilitate the reality of our flexible, ever-changing world. P^2M^2 was also designed understanding that the future is not always predictable and recognizes that the overall goal for a project is a satisfied customer.

The traditional triangle of project success comprised three variables: cost, schedule, and quality. A change in any variable caused changes in the other two variables. The new paradigm encompassed by P^2M^2 also includes people who are the focus of all activities:

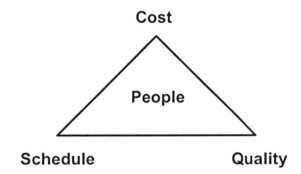

If project monies are reduced, the quality and/or project scope may suffer. If schedule is reduced, both quality (decreased to meet the new schedule) and cost (increased to maintain quality and meet the new schedule) may be affected. If the number of people is reduced, all other variables – schedule, quality, and cost – are affected.

The project manager is the key person responsible for managing people, cost, schedule, and quality for the project. The project manager also takes the lead role of defining goals (typically not measurable) and objectives (typically measurable), developing project plans, ensuring efficiency (resources are properly used) and effectiveness (customer is happy) of the project.

Typically, the major players in a project are:

- project sponsor
- project manager
- project team
- client (customer)
- senior management
- client review committee
- project steering committees

1. Project Sponsor

The project sponsor is assigned to a project by senior management. The sponsor is ultimately responsible for the overall success of the project. Some of the key responsibilities of the project sponsor are assigning the project manager, establishing the business objectives of the project in ensuring that these are met, acquiring sufficient resources to insure the success of the projects, citing legal contracts, reviewing and resolving funding requirements that are outside the project commitments, reviewing and resolving decisions and change requests, authorizing all changes to the statement of work, signing off on key project deliverables, and executing the final sign off for the project.

2. Project Manager

The project manager has direct responsibility for managing the delivery of the project as identified in the statement of work. Some of the key roles and responsibilities of the project manager are successfully completing the project, understanding the customer requirements, understanding and managing the project within the scope identified in the statement of work, managing the project to accomplish the goals and objectives identified in the statement of work, providing status reports to the project sponsor and other key stakeholders, identifying and acquiring resources necessary to complete the project, insuring the quality and content of all project deliverables, using change management practices to manage all changes to the project, and managing and controlling the project plan resources, quality and costs.

3. Project Team

The project team consists of individuals who complete tasks and produce deliverables for the project. Some of the key roles and responsibilities of the project team members are providing input to the planning process (in terms of tasks required, deliverables, and estimates), completing tasks as identified in the project plan, reporting status to the project manager, and identifying changes or decisions as early as possible.

4. Client (Customer)

The client represents the persons or organizations that will be the recipients of the project deliverables. Some of the key roles and responsibilities of the client are providing input on the client requirements, providing the team enough information to ensure success, reviewing all deliverables produced by the team, participating in acceptance testing of deliverables, and signing off on deliverables.

5. Senior Management

Senior management is responsible for determining which projects will be initiated. On specific projects, some of the key roles and responsibilities of senior management are advising the project sponsor, reviewing and resolving any project-related issues that are directed to senior management, and considering the impact of the project on other corporate projects and activities.

6. Client Review Committee

The client review committee is formed for some projects to review project deliverables and to provide client acceptance to the project. This committee is common on large projects or projects were the deliverables will be utilized across multiple organizations. Some of the key roles and responsibilities of the client review committee are providing executive input on business requirements, reviewing project deliverables, testing project deliverables, and signing off on project deliverables.

7. Project Steering Committee

The project steering committee is used for some projects to provide direction to the project team. This committee is usually formed on large projects or projects that affect multiple departments, divisions, or organizations. Some of the key roles and responsibilities of the project steering committee are reviewing project status, insuring the project is within the scope, providing guidance on issues related to risk management, reviewing and resolving appropriate project decision requests, and reviewing and advising on project change requests.

Appendices

Following is the P^{2}M^2 Overview Framework.

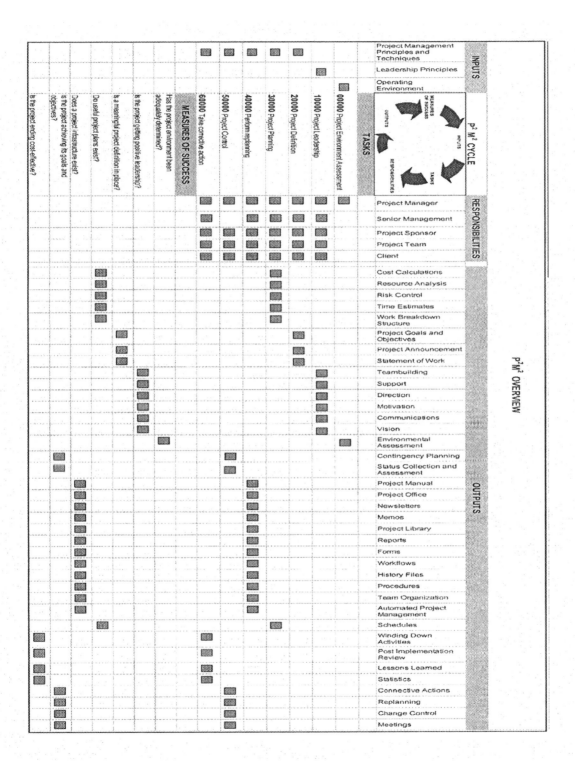

Appendix E. NASA SEL Dos and Don'ts for Software Success

Nine NASA SEL "Dos" for Software Success

<u>Create and follow a software development plan</u>

At the beginning of a project, prepare a software development plan that describes the project's vision, defines the team structure, and defines the development methods. The plan should include estimates, major milestones, and other measures that will be used to track progress. The software development plan should be a living document that is updated at the end of each major phase or stage.

<u>Empower project personnel</u>

Tap into the project team skill and potential by aligning the development team members with project vision, providing the members with a productive environment to work in, and assigning them clear responsibilities and the authority needed to carry out their responsibilities.

<u>Minimize the bureaucracy</u>

Establish the minimum amount of process overhead needed to satisfy the project's objectives. Be sure that there is a good reason for required meetings and paperwork. As NASA says, "Machines plus more documentation plus more management is not equal to more success."

<u>Define the requirements baseline, and manage changes to it</u>

Stabilize requirements as early as possible. Keep a detailed list of potentially volatile requirements or undefined requirements, and prioritize the list by estimated cost and schedule impact. Try to resolve these items during architecture or, at the latest, during detailed design.

Take periodic snapshots of project health and progress, and re-plan when necessary

Regularly compare the project's progress against the project plan and against similar past projects. If progress deviates significantly from the project plan, re-plan. Carefully consider reducing the scope of the work when re-planning, and try not to be unrealistically optimistic.

Re-estimate system size, effort, and schedules periodically

Each new phase of the project provides new information about the software being built. Do not insist on maintaining the original estimates; instead, plan to refine the estimates at the completion of each major milestone. Estimation is an inexact science, and there is nothing wrong with finding that the development team underestimated the project's size or overestimated its own productivity. What is wrong is not planning to periodically check an estimate accuracy and not correcting the estimates as the project progresses.

Define and manage phase transitions

Some projects lose time in the transition from requirements development to architecture, architecture to stage planning, the end of one stage to the beginning of the next, and so on. The project team should begin preliminary work on the next phase a few weeks before completing the current phase so that the team as a whole can make an efficient transition to the next phase.

Foster a team spirit

Even with a project that includes people from different organizations or companies, emphasize the common vision that every person on the project is working toward. Clearly define each person's individual responsibilities, but emphasize the whole-project context for which those responsibilities exist. Be sure to communicate status, risks, and other management issues throughout the project in the same way.

Start the project with a small senior staff

Begin the project with a small group of experienced senior people who will provide leadership throughout the project. Be sure they establish a vision, define the software concept, develop an approach to the project, and are generally in alignment with one another before junior staff is brought on board.

Eight NASA SEL "Don'ts" for Software Success

Don't let team members work in an unsystematic way

Efficient development of high quality software is not a touchy-feely, unmanageable process. It is a creative process, but one that benefits from a recent application of defined principles, practices, methods, and techniques. Insist that the team use systematic development practices.

Don't set unreasonable goals

Setting unreasonable goals is worse than setting no goals at all. If the team members don't believe in the goals, they will merely put in their time, punch the clock, and go home. If they are rushed, they will make mistakes upstream that cost fortunes to correct downstream. Set reasonable, moderately challenging goals, and the team will stretch to meet them without damaging project efficiency.

Don't implement changes without assessing their impact and obtaining approval of the change board

Estimate the impact of each change – even important, small changes that the project can absorb without rescheduling. The project needs a record of how much changed over time, both in major and minor ways. Even when a particular change does not have a large impact, small changes add up over time and will eventually cause cost and schedule overruns if not controlled.

Don't gold plate

Implement only what is required. Developers, managers, and customers often think of small, easy changes that seem to make the software better. However, these changes often have much more far-reaching impact than anticipated by the specific developer who implemented the change. Do not let additional complexity creep into the project through gold plating.

Don't overstaff, especially early in the project

Start the project with a small senior team. Bring additional people on to the project only when there is meaningful work for them to do. This guideline does allow for some early use of junior personnel to establish requirements and early architecture. Relatively junior staff members can review documents, investigate capabilities of tools including libraries, and perform many other tasks requiring good technical skills but not guru-level standing.

Don't assume that a schedule slip in the middle of a phase will be made up later

A common mistake is to assume that productivity will improve as the project progresses from the beginning of a phase to the end. Productivity might improve slightly, but there isn't enough time within any particular phase to make up time. More generally, do not assume that a schedule slip at any point in the project will be made up later. If the project doesn't catch up soon after a slip is detected, you can safely assume that it won't be possible to catch up.

Don't relax standards in order to cut costs or shorten a schedule

Relaxing standards tends to introduce errors into the project, and optimum project cost and schedule both depend on eliminating errors. Relaxing standards can also have a de-motivating effect. Most developers are quality oriented, and the relaxation of standards sends the message that the customer or upper management doesn't care about quality.

Don't assume that a large amount of documentation insures success

Different projects require different kinds of documentation support. The optimum amount and kind of documentation required is based on the project size, schedule, and expected lifetime of the system. Avoid the United States Department of Defense style documentation in which a 25,000 line of code program could easily require 5,000 to 10,000 pages of paperwork, and a 100,000 line of code program could require as many as 40,000 pages of paperwork.

(McConnell, 1998)

Appendix F. Query Definition Template - LDSALES

```
Query: LDSALES       Library: SALESLIB        Query Definition Template                    Page    1
10/25/05 11:21:20    6.4    1040630 - PTF03 050110

Created by. . . . . . BULLREY       Last update by. . . . JMANNING       Last Run by . . . . . BULLREY
Created on Date . . . 2/09/05       Last Query Update . . 9/17/05        Last Query Run. . . . 10/20/05
                                    Number of updates . .     20         Number of runs. . . .     591
```

```
Data Source Files:
    3 Files found
File        Record      Library    Member     File                                            File Level        Alias for
Name        Format      Name                  Description                                     Identifier        File

ALL_SALES   ALLSALESR   BRULIB     *METAFILE  SoftPak sales for all customers                 1051024160337
    Actual files used for dictionary view: ALL_SALES   Format: ALLSALESR   Library: BRULIB
            File        Record      Library    Member     File                                File Level
            Name        Format      Name                  Description                          Identifier
            PRALLCUST   IQOUTPUT    SPTEST     *FIRST      Output file for BRULIB/BLPLSTCUS     1050104231426
CUSTOMER    CUSTOMERR   BRULIB     *METAFILE  Meta file for the customer master file          1051024160337
    Actual files used for dictionary view: CUSTOMER    Format: CUSTOMERR   Library: BRULIB
            File        Record      Library    Member     File                                File Level
            Name        Format      Name                  Description                          Identifier
            PRCUST      IQOUTPUT    SPTEST     *FIRST      Output file for BRULIB/CPYCUST       1040202110213
CONTRACTS   CONTRACTSR  BRULIB     *METAFILE  Soft-Pak Contract Master File                   1051024160337
    Actual files used for dictionary view: CONTRACTS   Format: CONTRACTSR   Library: BRULIB
            File        Record      Library    Member     File                                File Level
            Name        Format      Name                  Description                          Identifier
            PRCPRH      IQOUTPUT    SPTEST     *FIRST      Output file for BRULIB/CPYCPRH       1040209152714
```

```
File Join Structure:
    4 Joins found
File        Record      Library    Field                                                          Field
Name        Format      Name       Name                                                           Name

ALL_SALES   ALLSALESR   BRULIB     COMPANY                                                         F02.COMPANY_ID
ALL_SALES   ALLSALESR   BRULIB     CUST_NU                                                         CUSTOMER_NBR
ALL_SALES   ALLSALESR   BRULIB     COMPANY                                                         COMPANY_CODE
ALL_SALES   ALLSALESR   BRULIB     CUST_NU                                                         CUST_NBR
```

> **Eight user defined new fields that should have been created in a COPY or BUILD query, not in a LOAD query!**

```
New Fields:
    8 New Fields Found
Field           Length Decimals Column
Name                            Headings        Calculation:

LOB_TYPE        2           C   LOB Type        %SUBSTRING(F02.TYPSRC 1 2)
PRICE_CODE      2           C   Price Code      %SUBSTRING(F02.TYPSRC 5 2)
SIZ_CHG_1       1           C   Size Code Pos 1 %SUBSTRING(SIZE_CODE 1 1)
SIZ_CHG_2       1           C   Size Code Pos 2 %SUBSTRING(SIZE_CODE 2 1)
SIZ_CHG_3       1           C   Charge Code Pos 1 %SUBSTRING(CHARGE_CODE 1 1)
SIZ_CHG_4       1           C   Charge Code Pos 2 %SUBSTRING(CHARGE_CODE 2 1)
PLIST_POS1      1           C   Price List Pos 1 %SUBSTRING(PRICE_LIST 1 1)
RCD_COUNT       8       0   P   Record Counter  1
```

```
Query: LDSALES       Library: SALESLIB        Query Definition Template                    Page    2
10/25/05 11:21:25    6.4    1040630 - PTF03 050110
```

```
Sequenced/Formatted Fields:
    50 Sequenced Fields Found
File        Record      Library    Field         Column               Fld Dec Original Fld Edit  Field Heading   Field       Print Round
Name        Format      Name       Name          Heading              Len Pos Len Pos Type Code  Lin Pos Pos     Spacing when Used

ALL_SALES   ALLSALESR   BRULIB     MARKET_NAME   Market Name          15      15       C                          1  Always
ALL_SALES   ALLSALESR   BRULIB     DISTRICT      District Code         3       3       C                          1  Always
ALL_SALES   ALLSALESR   BRULIB     DISTRICT_NAME District Name        25      25       C                          1  Always
ALL_SALES   ALLSALESR   BRULIB     PROFIT_CENTER Profit Center         3       3       C                          1  Always
ALL_SALES   ALLSALESR   BRULIB     COMPANY       Company Number        2       2       C                          1  Always
ALL_SALES   ALLSALESR   BRULIB     COMPANY_NAME  Company Name         25      25       C                          1  Always
ALL_SALES   ALLSALESR   BRULIB     CUST_NUMBER   Sale Customer Number  5   3   5   0   S    J                      1  Always
ALL_SALES   ALLSALESR   BRULIB     CUST_NAME     Customer Name        25      25       C                          1  Always
CUSTOMER    CUSTOMERR   BRULIB     START_DATE    Start Date            8   0   8   0   S    J                      1  Always
CUSTOMER    CUSTOMERR   BRULIB     STOP_DATE     Stop Date             8   0   8   0   S    J                      1  Always
ALL_SALES   ALLSALESR   BRULIB     PERM_OR_TEMP  Detection Flag        1       1       C                          1  Always
CUSTOMER    CUSTOMERR   BRULIB     RES_CUSTOMER  Residential Customer  1       1       C                          1  Always
CUSTOMER    CUSTOMERR   BRULIB     BILL_CYCLE    Bill Cycle            2       2       C                          1  Always
ALL_SALES   ALLSALESR   BRULIB     WORK_ORDER_NBR Work Order Number    7   0   7   0   P    3                      1  Always
ALL_SALES   ALLSALESR   BRULIB     SIZE_CODE     Size Code             2       2       C                          1  Always
ALL_SALES   ALLSALESR   BRULIB     CHARGE_CODE   Charge Code           2       2       C                          1  Always
ALL_SALES   ALLSALESR   BRULIB     DATE_POSTED   Posted Date           8   0   8   0   S    J                      1  Always
                                                                    Edit Word:   6 / / /
ALL_SALES   ALLSALESR   BRULIB     YEAR_AND_MONTH Year and Month       6   0   6   0   P    Y                      1  Always
ALL_SALES   ALLSALESR   BRULIB     SALE_DESCRIPTN Sale Description     35      35       C                          1  Always
ALL_SALES   ALLSALESR   BRULIB     F01_TYPSRC    TYPSRC               10      10       C                          1  Always
ALL_SALES   ALLSALESR   BRULIB     F01_SALES_PERS Sales Person        10      10       C                          1  Always
ALL_SALES   ALLSALESR   BRULIB     BUSINESS_TYPE Business Type         2       2       C                          1  Always
                                   PRICE_CODE    Price Code            2       2       C                          2  Always
                                   PLIST_POS1    Price List Pos 1      1       1       C                          2  Always
ALL_SALES   ALLSALESR   BRULIB     PRICE_LIST    Price List            4       4       C                          1  Always
ALL_SALES   ALLSALESR   BRULIB     PRICE_LIST_DES Price List Desc.    25      25       C                          1  Always
ALL_SALES   ALLSALESR   BRULIB     QUANTITY      Quantity              7   2   7   2   P    3                      1  Always
ALL_SALES   ALLSALESR   BRULIB     AMOUNT_BILLED Amount Billed         9   2   9   2   P    3                      1  Always
ALL_SALES   ALLSALESR   BRULIB     SERVICE_TYPE  Service Type Code     2       2       C                          1  Always
CUSTOMER    CUSTOMERR   BRULIB     BILL_ADDR_1   Billing Address 1    25      25       C                          2  Always
CUSTOMER    CUSTOMERR   BRULIB     BILL_ADDR_2   Billing Address 2    25      25       C                          2  Always
CUSTOMER    CUSTOMERR   BRULIB     BILL_CITY     Billing City         15      15       C                          2  Always
CUSTOMER    CUSTOMERR   BRULIB     BILL_STATE    Billing State         3       3       C                          2  Always
CUSTOMER    CUSTOMERR   BRULIB     BILL_ZIP      Billing Zip           9       9       C                          2  Always
ALL_SALES   ALLSALESR   BRULIB     GL_COMPANY    G/L Company           3       3       C                          1  Always
ALL_SALES   ALLSALESR   BRULIB     GL_ABBRV_CODE Abbrv. G/L Code       3       3       C                          1  Always
ALL_SALES   ALLSALESR   BRULIB     LOB_FROM_GLNBR LOB Code from G/L    7       7       C                          1  Always
ALL_SALES   ALLSALESR   BRULIB     GL_NUMBER     G/L Number           25      25       C                          1  Always
ALL_SALES   ALLSALESR   BRULIB     GL_DESC_1     GL Description 1     25      25       C                          1  Always
ALL_SALES   ALLSALESR   BRULIB     GL_DESC_2     GL description 2     25      25       C                          1  Always
                                   SIZ_CHG_1     Size Code Pos 1       1       1       C                          2  Always
                                   SIZ_CHG_2     Size Code Pos 2       1       1       C                          2  Always
                                   SIZ_CHG_3     Charge Code Pos 1     1       1       C                          2  Always
                                   SIZ_CHG_4     Charge Code Pos 2     1       1       C                          2  Always
CONTRACTS   CONTRACTSR  BRULIB     CONTRACT_ID   Contract ID          10      10       C                          1  Always
CONTRACTS   CONTRACTSR  BRULIB     EFFECTIVE_DATE Effective Date       8   0   8   0   S    J                      1  Always
```

173

Query: LOSALES   Library: SALESLIB   Query Definition Template   Page   3
10/25/05 11:21:20   6.4   1040630 - PTF03 050110

Sequenced/Formatted Fields:
  50 Sequenced Fields Found

File Name	Record Format	Library Name	Field Name	Column Heading	Fld Len	Dec Pos	Original Fld Len	Fld Pos	Edit Type	Field Code	Heading Lin Pos	Field Pos	Print Spacing When	Round Used
CONTRACTS	CONTRACTSR	BRULIB	EXPIRE_DATE	Expiration Date	8	0	8		S	J			1	Always
ALL_SALES	ALLSALESR	BRULIB	ACCOUNT_PERIOD	Acct. Period	6	0	6		S	J			1	Always
ALL_SALES	ALLSALESR	BRULIB	BILL_PERIOD	Unbilled per yyyy/mm	6	0	6		S	J			1	Always
			RCD_COUNT	Record Counter	6	0	9		P	J			2	Always

Record Selection:
  23 Record Selections Found

And File /Or Name	Record Format	Library Name	Test Field Name	Operator	Test Value
	ALL_SALES	ALLSALESR	BRULIB	MARKET_NAME	LIST ?

Comments: Enter an optional list of Market Names. Use 'Central Oh' 'Cincinnati' 'Corporate' 'Northwest' 'Southeast' 'Southern' 'Discontinued' 'League' 'Pumpke National'. Use upper and lower case exactly as shown above. Use single quotes with a space between each entry. Press continue with no entry to select all markets.

AND ALL_SALES ALLSALESR BRULIB ACCOUNT_PERIOD RANGE   ?
Comments: format. For example, 200503 200505 would select sales from February through May, 2005. Do not use quotes, but leave a space between each entry. Enter a year and month range for desired sales records. Use CCYYMM

AND ALL_SALES ALLSALESR BRULIB COMPANY LIST   ?
Comments: quotes with a space between each entry. Alpha IDs are upper case. Enter an optional list of SoftPak company IDs to INCLUDE. Use single For example: '01' '02' 'T1'

AND ALL_SALES ALLSALESR BRULIB COMPANY NLIST   ?
Comments: For example: '01' '02' 'T1'. Enter an optional list of SoftPak company IDs to EXCLUDE. Use single quotes with a space between each entry. Alpha IDs are upper case.

AND CUSTOMER CUSTOMERR BRULIB RES_CUSTOMER LIST   ?
Comments: Press continue with no entry to select both. Enter 'N' to INCLUDE Commercial customers only. Enter 'Y' to INCLUDE Residential customers only.

AND CUSTOMER CUSTOMERR BRULIB START_DATE RANGE   ?
Comments: Enter an optional range of customer start dates. Use CCYYMMDD format. Do not use quotes. For example, use 20040701 20041231 to select customers starting from July 1, 2004 through December 31, 2004.

AND CONTRACTS CONTRACTSR BRULIB EXPIRE_DATE RANGE   ?
Comments: billing customers. NOTE: Municiple subscription billing customers quotes. Leave a space between each date. Use YYYYMMDD format. must also have a price list beginning with an '*' Enter an optional range of contract expiration dates. Do not use For example: 20401231 20401231 will select Municiple Subscription

AND ALL_SALES ALLSALESR BRULIB CUST_NUMBER LIST   ?
Comments: customer numbers. Do not use quotes. Leave a space between each customer number.

Query: LOSALES   Library: SALESLIB   Query Definition Template   Page   4
10/25/05 11:21:20   6.4   1040630 - PTF03 050110

Record Selection:
  23 Record Selections Found

And File /Or Name	Record Format	Library Name	Test Field Name	Operator	Test Value

Press enter with no entry to INCLUDE all customers or enter a list of

AND ALL_SALES ALLSALESR BRULIB CUST_NAME LIKE   ?
Comments: You may enter a partial customer name. For example '%BIGFOOT%' would select customers with BIGFOOT anywhere in their name. Use quotes and percent signs exactly as shown. This is an optional entry.

AND CUSTOMER CUSTOMERR BRULIB BILL_ADDR_2 LIKE   ?
Comments: shown. This entry is to find OAKLEAF customers. Enter '%OAK%'. This selects from billing address line 2. Use quotes and percent sign exactly as

AND PLIST_POS1 LIST   ?
Comments: Enter an optional list taken from the first position of a Price List code. Use single quotes with a space between each entry. For example: '*' 'B'

AND ALL_SALES ALLSALESR BRULIB PRICE_LIST LIST   ?
Comments: Enter an optional list of Price List codes to INCLUDE. Use single quotes with a space between each entry. For example: 'CIN' '*WAS'

AND PRICE_CODE LIST   ?
Comments: with a space between each entry. For example: 'A1' 'N1'. Enter an optional list of Price Codes to INCLUDE. Use single quotes

AND CUSTOMER CUSTOMERR BRULIB BILL_CYCLE LIST   ?
Comments: with a space between each entry. For example: 'Q1' 'Q2' 'Q3'. Enter an optional list of Bill Cycles to INCLUDE. Use single quotes

AND LOB_TYPE LIST   ?
Comments: Enter an optional list of LOB types to INCLUDE. Use single quotes with a space between each entry. For example: 'RF' 'FL' 'RO'

AND LOB_TYPE NLIST   ?
Comments: Enter an optional list of LOB types to EXCLUDE. Use single quotes with a space between each entry. For example: 'RF' 'FL' 'RO'

AND ALL_SALES ALLSALESR BRULIB GL_ABBRV_CODE LIST   ?
Comments: For example: 'XXXXX' 'YYYYY' 'ZZZZZ'. Use single quotes with a space between each entry. Enter and optional list of G/L Abbreviated codes to INCLUDE.

AND ALL_SALES ALLSALESR BRULIB SIZE_CODE LIST   ?
Comments: with a space between each entry. For example: 'UO' 'UR'. Enter an optional list of Size Codes to INCLUDE. Use single quotes

AND ALL_SALES ALLSALESR BRULIB CHARGE_CODE LIST   ?
Comments: with a space between each entry. For example: 'A1' 'A5'. Enter an optional list of Charge Codes to INCLUDE. Use single quotes

AND SIZ_CHG_1 LIST   ?
Comments: Use single quotes with a space between each entry. For example: 'J' 'K' 'L' 'M'. Enter and optional list of codes from size code position 1.

AND SIZ_CHG_2 LIST   ?
Comments: Use single quotes with a space between each entry. For example: 'A' 'B' 'F' 'G'. Enter and optional list of codes from size code position 2.

AND SIZ_CHG_3 LIST   ?

Query: LOSALES   Library: SALESLIB   Query Definition Template   Page   5
10/25/05 11:21:20   6.4   1040630 - PTF03 050110

Record Selection:
  23 Record Selections Found

And File /Or Name	Record Format	Library Name	Test Field Name	Operator	Test Value

Comments: Use single quotes with a space between each entry. For example: 'A' 'B' 'F' 'G'. Enter and optional list of codes from charge code position 1.

AND SIZ_CHG_4 LIST   ?
Comments: For example: 'A' 'B' 'C' 'D'. Enter and optional list of codes from charge code position 2. Use single quotes with a space between each entry.

Sort Fields:
  3 Sort Sequence Fields Found

File Name	Record Format	Library Name	Field Name	Descend	Ignore Sign
ALL_SALES	ALLSALESR	BRULIB	MARKET_NAME		
ALL_SALES	ALLSALESR	BRULIB	COMPANY		
ALL_SALES	ALLSALESR	BRULIB	CUST_NUMBER		

Appendices

Query Processing Options:

- -

Output Specifications:

```
Output Device and Type Options:
  Output . . . . . . . . . . . . . Display Report
  Type of Output . . . . . . . . . Detail
  Send output when complete. . . . .
```

Query Processing Options:

- -

```
Query Run Options:
  Return Records with Missing Fields. . . . . Yes
  Number of Unique Key Fields . . . . . . . . None
  Number of Records to Query. . . . . . . . . All Records
  Query to Run Next . . . . . . . . .
    Library of Query to Run Next . . . . . .
    Maximum number of links. . . . . . . .      10
  Ignore Numeric Field Errors . . . . . . . . No
  Integrate tables with totals. . . . . . . . Yes
  Run Environment . . . . . . . . . . . . . . Both
```

- -

```
Query Run Attributes:
  Query Optimization Type. . . . . . Determine at Run Time
  Consider All Access Paths. . . . . Yes
  Create Temporary Results . . . . . If Needed
  Return Status Messages . . . . . . Yes
  Ignore Case Fields for Sort Fields No
  Join Order for Files . . . . . . . Any Order
  Interface Type . . . . . . . . . . Direct
  Allow precision reduction. . . . . No
  Null processing method . . . . . . Keep Values
  Use IDDU Definitions . . . . . . . Yes
  Any IDDU Files Used. . . . . . . . No
```

- -

```
Submitted Job Description Overrides.
  Job Name . . . . . . . . . . . . . *QUERY
  Job Description Name . . . . . . . *USRPRF
    Job Description Library Name . .
  Job Queue Name . . . . . . . . . . *JOBD
    Job Queue Library Name . . . . .
  Print Text . . . . . . . . . . . . *CURRENT
  Output Queue Name. . . . . . . . . *CURRENT
    Output Queue Library Name. . . .
  Hold on Job Queue. . . . . . . . . *JOBD
  Allow Display by DSPSBMJOB . . . . Yes
```

- -

```
Query Descriptions:
  Query Text . . . . . . . . . . . Load Customer Sales from 7/01/03 forward to Qport
  Print Text . . . . . . . . . . . *CURRENT
  Query Authority. . . . . . . . . Change
```

175

Appendix G. Author's User Manual Table of Contents

Rumpke Consolidated Companies Data Warehouse
User Instructions

Table of Contents

Appendices

Appendix H. Dr. Kerzner's 16 Points to Project Management Maturity

1. Adopt a project management methodology and use it consistently.

2. Implement a philosophy that drives the company toward project management maturity and communicate it to everyone.

3. Commit to developing effective plans at the beginning of each project.

4. Minimize scope changes by committing to realistic objectives.

5. Recognize that cost and schedule management are inseparable.

6. Select the right person as the project manager.

7. Provide executives with project sponsor information, not project management information.

8. Strengthen involvement and support of line management.

9. Focus on deliverables rather than resources.

10. Cultivate effective communication, cooperation, and trust to achieve rapid project management maturity.

11. Share recognition for project success with the entire project team and line management.

12. Eliminate non-productive meetings.

13. Focus on identifying and solving problems early, quickly, and cost effectively.

14. Measure progress periodically.

15. Use project management software as a tool – not as a substitute for effective planning or interpersonal skills.

16. Institute an all-employee training program with periodic updates based upon documented lessons learned.

Kerzner (2001)

Appendix I. DW Developers' Stress Reduction Kit

Stress Reduction Kit

Bang Head Here

Directions:
1. Place kit on FIRM surface.
2. Follow directions in circle of kit.
3. Repeat step 2 as necessary, or until unconscious.
4. If unconscious, cease stress reduction activity.

Appendix J. 30 Things We Know for Sure About Training (Condensed)

The following is a condensed version of Ron and Susan Zemke's "30 Things We Know for Sure About Adult Learning" (1988):

We don't know a lot about the mechanisms of adult learning. At least, not in the "What are the minimum – necessary and sufficient – conditions for infecting a permanent change in an adult's behavior?" sense of knowing. In that, we are not alone. Malcolm Knowles came to much the same conclusion in *The Adult Learner: A Neglected Species*. Eight years ago, he equated his efforts to summarize what was then known about adult learning to a trip up the Amazon: "It is a strange world that we're going to explore together, with lush growth of flora and fauna with exotic names (including fossils of extinct species) and teaming with savage tribes in raging battle. I have just made a casing-the-joint trip up the river myself, and I can tell you that my head is reeling." Today, Knowles says, "The river is much tamer. We are beginning to understand what we do that works and why it works." But as we listen, we have the distinct impression that what our point man Knowles sees as tame travel can still be white-water rapids for the rest of us.

While there are hundreds of books and articles offering tips and tricks for teaching adults, the bulk of that knowledge is derived from three relatively limited spheres. The first is "My life and times in teaching," wherein one teacher/trainer of adults shares his or her career's accumulation of secrets with others. Though intriguing and interesting, this literature focuses more on teacher survival than anything else. While we learn much about living, we learn relatively little about learning. The second common source is the "Why adults decide to study" research. Here we learn some interesting, even fascinating, things about the conditions and incidents that motivate adults to engage in a "focused learning effort." But in most of this research, the adult seems assumed to be a learning machine who, once switched on, vacuums up knowledge and skill. It is more indicative then instructive, more suggestive than substantive. A cynic would call this body of knowledge about adult learning a form of market research. The third source is extrapolation from theory – both adult learning theory and research – derived from work with children and nonhuman subjects. The adult learning theories in question are really holistic treatments of human nature: The Carl Rogers/Abraham Maslow sort of theories from which we can only infer, or guess at, rules of practice. "Would you rather learn from a lecture or a book?" or "On your own with direction?" are interesting questions, but ones that beg the issue of results or learning outcomes. A trainee may prefer listening to lectures but learn best buy practice and application exercises.

The non adult theory in research is a broad lot – everything from child development studies to pigeon training. The tendency seems to be to draw guidance from the B.F. Skinner/behavior modification/programmed instruction, and the Albert Bandura/behavior modeling/social learning schools of thought. While both schools are generating research and results, they are still shorter on proven practices then pontification and speculation. No single theory, or set of theories, seems to have an arm-lock on understanding adults or helping us work effectively and efficiently with them.

Still in all, from a variety of sources there emerges a body of fairly reliable knowledge about adult learning – arbitrarily, 30 points that lend themselves to three basic divisions:

- Things we know about adult learners and their motivation.
- Things we know about designing curricula for adults.
- Things we know about working with adults in the classroom.

These are not be-all, end-all categories. They overlap more than just a little bit. But they help us understand what we're learning from others about adult learning.

Motivation to Learn

Adult learners can't be threatened, coerced or tricked into learning something new. Birch rods and gold stars have minimum impact. Adults can be ordered into a classroom and prodded into a seat, but they cannot be forced to learn. Though trainers are often faced with adults who have been sent to training, there are some insights to be garnered from the research on adults who seek out a structured learning experience on their own. It's something we all do at least twice a year, the research says. We begin our running tally from this base camp.

1. Adults seek out learning experiences in order to cope with specific life-changing events. Marriage, divorce, a new job, a promotion, being fired, retiring, losing a loved one and moving into a new city are examples.

2. The more life-change events an adult encounters, the more likely he or she is to seek out learning opportunities. Just as stress increases as life-change events accumulate, the motivation to cope with change through engagement in a learning experience increases. Since the people who most frequently seek out learning opportunities are people who have the most overall years of education, it is reasonable to guess that for many of us learning is a coping response to significant change.

3. The learning experiences adults seek out on their own are directly related – at least in their own perceptions – to the life-change events that triggered the seeking. Therefore, if 80% of the change being encountered is work related, than 80% of the adult learning experiences sought should be work related.

4. Adults are generally willing to engage in learning exercises before, after or even during the actual life change event. Once convinced that the change is a certainty, adults will engage in any learning that promises to help them cope with the transition.

5. Although adults have been found to engage in learning for a variety of reasons – job advancement, pleasure, love of learning and so on – it is equally true that for most adults learning is not its own reward. Adults who are motivated to seek out a learning experience do so primarily (80 – 90% of the time) because they have a use for the knowledge or skill being sought. Learning is a means to an end, not an end in itself.

6. Increasing or maintaining one's sense of self-esteem and pleasure are strong secondary motivators for engaging in learning experiences. Having a new skill or extending and enriching current knowledge can be both, depending on the individual's personal perceptions.

Curriculum Design

7. Adult learners tend to be less interested in, and enthralled by, survey courses. They tend to prefer single-concept, single-theory courses that focus heavily on the application of the concept to relevant problems. This tendency increases with age.

8. Adults need to be able to integrate new ideas with what they already know if they're going to keep – and use – the new information.

9. Information that conflicts sharply with what is already held to be true, and thus forces a re-evaluation of the old material, is integrated more slowly.

10. Information that has little "conceptual overlap" with what is already known is acquired slowly.

11. Fast-paced, complex or unusual learning tasks interfere with the learning of the concepts or data they are intended to teach or illustrate.

12. Adults tend to compensate for being slower in some psychomotor learning tasks by being more accurate and making fewer trial-and-error ventures.

13. Adults tend to take errors personally and are more likely to let them affect self-esteem. Therefore, they tend to apply tried-and-true solutions and take fewer risks. There is even evidence that adults will misinterpret feedback and "mistake" errors for positive confirmation.

14. The curriculum designer must know whether the concepts and ideas will be in concert or in conflict with learner and organizational values. As trainers at AT&T have learned, moving from a service to sales philosophy requires more than a change in words and titles. It requires a change in the way people think and value.

15. Programs need to be designed to accept viewpoints from people in different life stages and with different value "sets."

16. A concept needs to be "anchored" or explained from more than one value set and appeal to more than one developmental life stage.

17. Adults prefer self-directed and self-designed learning objectives seven to one over group-learning exercises led by a professional.

18. Nonhuman media such as books, program instruction and television have become popular in recent years. One piece of research found them very influential in the way adults plan self-directed learning projects.

19. Regardless of media, straightforward how-to is the preferred content orientation. As many as 80% of older adults in one study cited the need for application and how-to information as the primary motivation for undertaking a learning project.

20. Self-direction does not mean isolation. In fact, studies of self-directed learning show self-directed projects involve an average of ten other people as resources, guides, encouragers and the like. The incompetence or inadequacy of these same people is often rated as a primary frustration.

In The Classroom

21. The learning environment must be physically and psychologically comfortable. Adults report that long lectures, periods of interminable sitting, and the absence of practice opportunities are high on the irritation scale.

22. Adults have something real to lose in a classroom situation. Self-esteem and ego are on the line when they're asked to risk trying a new behavior in front of peers and cohorts. Bad experiences in traditional education, feelings about authority and preoccupation with events outside the classroom all affect in-class experience. These and other influencing factors are carried into class with the learners as surely as their gold cross pens and lined yellow pads.

23. Adults have expectations, and it is critical to take time up front to clarify and articulate all expectations before getting into content. Both the trainees and the instructor/facilitator need to state their expectations. When they are at variance, the problem should be acknowledged and a resolution negotiated. In any case, the instructor can assume responsibility only for his or her own expectations, not for the trainees.

24. Adults bring a great deal of life experience into the classroom, an invaluable asset to be acknowledged, tapped and used. Adults can learn well – and much – from dialogue with respected peers.

25. Instructors who have a tendency to hold forth rather than facilitate can hold that tendency in check – or compensate for it – by concentrating on the use of open-ended questions to draw out relevant trainee knowledge and experience.

26. New knowledge has to be integrated with previous knowledge; that means active learner participation. Since only the learners can tell us how the new fits or fails to fit with the old, we have to ask them. Just as the learner is dependent on us for confirming feedback on skill practice,

we are dependent on the learner for feedback about our curriculum and in class performance.

27. The key to the instructor's role is control. The instructor must balance the presentation of new material, debate and discussion, sharing of relevant trainee experiences and the clock. Ironically, we seem best able to establish control when we risk giving it up. When we shelve our egos and stifle the tendency to be threatened by challenge to our plans and methods, we gain the kind of facilitative control we seem to need to affect adult learning.

28. The instructor has to protect minority opinion, keep disagreements civil and unheated, make connections between various opinions and ideas, and keep reminding the group of the variety of potential solutions to the problem. Just as any good problem-solving meeting, the instructor is less advocate then orchestrator.

29. Integration of new knowledge and skill requires transition time and focused effort working on applications to specific back-on-the-job problems helps with the transfer. Action plans, accountability strategies and follow-up after training all increase the likelihood of that transfer. Involving the trainees supervisor in pre- and post-course activities helps with both in-class focus and transfer.

30. Learning and teaching theories function better as a resource than a Rosetta stone. The four currently influential theories – humanistic, behavioral, cognitive and developmental – all offer valuable guidance when matched with an appropriate learning task. A skill-training task can draw much from the behavioral approach, for example, while personal growth-centered subjects seem to draw gainfully from humanistic concepts. The trainer of adults needs to take an eclectic rather than a single theory-based approach to developing strategies and procedures.

Appendix K. A Statement of Work Template

 Rumpke
Consolidated
Companies

STATEMENT OF WORK (SOW) FOR SERVICES

Customer Information Management System

with

<NAME OF VENDOR>

for

Customer Information Management System Replacement System

September 28, 2006

	Rumpke		SOW for Services
	Consolidated		Rev. 1.0, 9/28/06
	Companies		

TABLE OF CONTENTS

Rumpke
Consolidated
Companies

1. Introduction

The purpose of this Statement of Work (SOW) is to detail the tasks and responsibilities of <VENDOR NAME> (hereinafter, the *Vendor*) in relation to the contract with Rumpke Consolidated Companies (hereinafter, the *Organization*) for <briefly DESCRIBE SERVICE>.

1.1 Background

<EXPLAIN WHY THE ORGANIZATION IS ACQUIRING THIS SERVICE> [*Example:* The Organization is contracting to provide for the services to remove the existing copier equipment and deploy a new fleet of equipment. The Vendor shall maintain the equipment per the <PROJECT NAME> Service Level Agreement.]

2. Scope

This SOW shall apply to the term stated in the <VENDOR NAME> contract. < DESCRIBE FULLY ALL WORK RELATED TO THIS CONTRACT> [*Example:*

- The contract goes into effect <DATE 1> and shall terminate on <DATE 2>.
- The current copier fleet shall be removed and transitioned into a new placement.
- The Vendor shall install 85 digital copiers per the attachment A (list of locations with monthly copy volumes) for the yearly cost of $<XXX,XXX.XX>.
- The contract includes all equipment, installation, removal, maintenance, upgrades and all supplies (excluding paper and staples).
- This SOW shall be done in the manner stated by the *Copier Program Service Level Agreement* agreed to by both the Vendor and the Organization.
- This statement of work is subject to all conditions and requirements of the initial bid by the Vendor.]

3. Tasks

3.1 General Requirements

- The Vendor shall submit a cost proposal with an associated project management plan addressing the tasks specified in the SOW
- Subtasks not specified in the SOW will be identified and include associated costs by project and task, milestones, and deliverable dates

**Rumpke
Consolidated
Companies**

- All written deliverables must be phrased in terms and language that can be easily understood by non-technical personnel (e.g., laypersons without subject matter expertise)

- All document deliverables must be in formats (hard copy and electronic) as specified by the customer/client - at a minimum, the formats must be in industry accepted standards (e.g., MS Word, MS PowerPoint, MS Project)

- The customer/client will complete a review of each submitted deliverable within specified working days for the date of receipt

- A kickoff meeting will be held at a location and time selected by the Organization where the Vendor and its staff will be introduced to the Organization.

- The Vendor and/or its staff must have knowledge and expertise of the environment (e.g., platforms, software, applications, network, tools, etc.) for which work is to be performed

- All items of this agreement shall be done in accordance with the <PROJECT NAME> Service Level Agreement.

3.2 Mandatory Tasks and Associate Deliverables

<LIST ALL MAJOR TASKS AND DELIVERABLES RELATED TO THIS PROJECT>
[*Example:*

3.2.1 *Removal of Existing Equipment*

- The Vendor shall remove all of the previous contracted equipment in preparation for deployment of the new equipment.

- A removal schedule shall be created to match the deployment schedule.

- The removal schedule shall be approved by the Organization's <PROJECT NAME> Project Manager before work begins removing any equipment.

- Deliverables:
  - Removal Schedule
  - Report of final meterage readings per device.

3.2.2 *Implementation/Conversion Plan*

- The Vendor shall deploy equipment as directed in Attachment A. The deployment shall include acquisition, Site readiness check, installation, configuration, and test.

- The Vendor shall present to the Organization's <PROJECT NAME> Project Manager an Implementation Schedule detailing deployment of devices listed in *Attachment A*.

- Deliverables:
  - Implementation Schedule tied to the Deployment List
  - Deployment List of devices with locations.

3.2.3 Training and Documentation Plan

- The Vendor shall provide a detailed training plan and schedule.
- Deliverables:
  - Training Schedule, matching the Deployment Schedule
  - Training Curriculum for Key Operators and Users

3.2.4 Maintenance, Warranty and Administration Requirements

- The Vendor shall provide a Maintenance, Warrantee and Administration Plan covering each type of device and the associated preventive maintenance program. All devices shall be maintained per the requirements of the <PROJECT NAME> Service Level Agreement.
- Deliverables:
  - Maintenance Plan
  - Warrantee Plan
  - Admin Plan

3.2.5 Reporting

- The Vendor shall provide reporting to the <PROJECT NAME> Program Manager on a <DEFINE REPORTING INTERVAL> [*Example: quarterly and yearly*> basis. The document shall report for each device: Service Standards, <LIST IMPORTANT PARAMETERS> [*Example: Device uptime, usage rates by account code and function, device downtime and service calls.*> <LIST FORMATS REQUIRED> [*Example: Reports shall be provided in MS Office format*>
- Deliverables:
  - Weekly Reports
  - Monthly Reports
  - Quarterly Reports
  - Annual Reports.

Rumpke Consolidated Companies

SOW for Services
Rev. 1.0, 9/28/06

3.2.6 Change Management Plan

- The Vendor shall provide a Change Management Plan to document procedures for additions, deletions and modifications to the <LIST ITEMS THAT MIGHT BE CHANGED>.
- Deliverables:
  - Procedures for Additions
  - Procedures for Modifications
  - Procedures for Deletions.

3.3 Contacts

- Provide the following points of contact with the following information.
- Administration Point of Contact
  - Name:
  - Command:
  - Agency:
  - Address (Include Office Symbol):
  - Phone: (DSN); (Commercial); (FAX)
  - E-Mail:
- Contracting Officer's Representative (COR).
  - Name:
  - Command:
  - Agency:
  - Address (Include Office Symbol):
  - Phone: (DSN); (Commercial); (FAX)
  - E-Mail:

4. Deliverables

4.1 Delivery Schedule

No.	Item	SOW Paragraph	Draft Due Date	Final Due Date	Recipient
1	Removal Schedule	3.2.1			
2	Implementation Schedule Tied to Deployment List	3.2.2			
3	Deployment List of Devices with Locations	3.2.2			
4	Training Schedule, Matching the Deployment Schedule	3.2.3			
5	Training Curriculum for Key Operators and Users	3.2.3			
6	Maintenance Plan	3.2.4			
7	Quarterly Reports	3.2.5			
8	Annual Reports	3.2.5			
9	Procedures for Additions	3.2.6			

10	Procedures for Modifications	3.2.6			
11	Procedures for Deletions	3.2.6			

- Deliverables must be provided on the dates specified in the proposal with associated project management plan. Any changes to the delivery date must have prior approval (in writing) by the <PROJECT NAME> Project Manager or designate.

- All deliverables must be submitted in a format approved by the customer/client contract official. At a minimum, the deliverable must be in an industry standard format - unless otherwise stipulated.

- If the deliverable cannot be provided within the scheduled time frame, the service provider is required to contact the <PROJECT NAME> Project Manager in writing with a reason for the delay and the proposed revised schedule. The request for a revised schedule must include the impact on related tasks and the overall project.

- A request for a revised schedule must be reviewed and approved by the <PROJECT NAME> Project Manager before placed in effect. Contract Terms and Conditions may dictate penalties, costs, and other actions based on the facts related to the request for a revised schedule.

4.2   Reports and Meetings

- The Vendor is required to provide the <PROJECT NAME> Project Manager with weekly written progress reports (one copy) of the implementation phase of this project. These are due to the <PROJECT NAME> Project Manager by the close of business (COB) on the last workday of the end of each calendar month throughout the life of the project

- The progress reports shall cover all work performed and completed during the week for which the progress report is provided and shall present the work to be performed during the subsequent week.

- The progress report shall identify any problems encountered or still outstanding with an explanation of the cause and resolution of the problem or how the problem will be resolved.

- The Vendor will be responsible for conducting weekly status meetings with the <PROJECT NAME> Project Manager. The meetings will be held on Monday of each week - at a time and place so designated by the <PROJECT NAME> Project Manager - unless revised by the <PROJECT NAME> Project Manager. The meetings can be in person or over the phone.

	Rumpke Consolidated Companies	SOW for Services Rev. 1.0, 9/28/06

5. Period and Place of Performance

5.1 Period of Performance

- The Vendor will conduct and complete the work associated with the contract at sites appropriate to the task and mutually agreed upon between the Vendor and the Organization.

- Mandatory tasks required under this SOW shall be completed in the specified number of calendar days or less from the date of the award - unless otherwise directed or agreed to by the <PROJECT NAME> Project Manager.

5.2 Place of Performance

- Mandatory tasks required under this SOW shall be completed in the specified location unless otherwise directed or agreed to by the <PROJECT NAME> Project Manager.

6. Payments

The Vendor shall invoice the Organization on a quarterly basis for payment on this statement of work. The invoice shall detail the each device, cost and the associated usage.

7. Vendor Personnel Requirements

The Vendor must have specialized experience and knowledge commensurate with the Organization's environment, device deployments and the specified task.

8. Customer/Client-Furnished Equipment and Work Space

- Depending on the nature of the task, the <PROJECT NAME> Project Manager will provide system access for on-site and off-site work - in accordance with established company policies, standards, regulations, and rules of conduct

- The <PROJECT NAME> Project Manager will provide the appropriate procedures, guidelines, standards, reference materials, and system/application documentation

- The <PROJECT NAME> Project Manager will provide access to the appropriate personnel (management, technical, subject matter expertise, etc.) necessary to fulfill the contract requirements.

Rumpke Consolidated Companies

9. Handling of Sensitive and/or Proprietary Information

- The Vendor will provide personnel who have signed or will sign a Non-Disclosure Agreement (NDA) or have been granted a classification clearance commensurate with the sensitivity of the tasks to be performed.

- Any information assets (company owned or custodial care) no longer required to complete the prescribed tasks must be returned to a designated Organization representative for storage or destruction. Unless approved by a designated Organization official, no sensitive or proprietary Organization information shall be removed, copies, or otherwise replicated from the Organization's site or domain.

10. Confidentiality and Non-Disclosure

- The preliminary and final deliverables as well as all associated working papers and other material considered relevant by the Organization's Contracting Official (CO) that have been generated by the Vendor in the performance of Organization business are the property of the Organization and must be submitted to the CO at the conclusion of the effort for evaluation, classification, and disposition.

- Access and use of the Organization's network shall be considered sensitive, on an as-required basis, and must be appropriately protected.

- All documents - hard copy or electronic - produced for this project are the property of the Organization. All appropriate project documentation will be given to the CO during and at the end of the contract. The Vendor will release no information without written permission from the Organization, or other designated official. Any request for information relating to this contract presented to the Vendor must be submitted to the CO for a response.

- The service provider personnel will be required to have a classification clearance commensurate with the sensitivity of the tasks to be performed. These personnel will be required to sign Non-Disclosure Statements and follow all provisions, restrictions, procedures, and policies commensurate to the tasks to be performed.

- Nothing herein shall be construed or applied in a manner inconsistent with *<Your state or province> Public Records Law, General Statutes .....*

11. Related Expenses

11.1 Travel

- All travel shall be the responsibility of the Vendor.
- Whenever possible, conference calls and video conferencing (when available and cost effective) should be used.

**Rumpke
Consolidated
Companies**

12. Signatures and Authorizations

The terms and conditions of the **Professional Services Agreement** apply in full to the services and products provided under this Statement of Work.

IN WITNESS WHEREOF, the parties hereto each acting with proper authority have executed this Statement of Work, under seal.

Client Full name	Service Provider Full name
Title	Title
Signature	Signature
Date	Date

Appendix L. A Sample of the User Manual

Record Selection for the LOB Data Mart Copies

SALESLIB:

CPYBCDE – Size and charge codes:	No selection needed
CPYBINS – Containers:	No selection needed
CPYBINSME – Containers:	No selection needed
CPYBINSMEP – Containers:	No selection needed
CPYCOCL – Commission Codes	No selection needed
CPYCOMP01 – Company File 01	No selection needed
CPYCPRD – Contract Detail	No selection needed
CPYCPRH – Contract Header	No selection needed
CPYCUST – Customer Master	No selection needed
CPYCUSTME – Customer Master	No selection needed
CPYCUSTMEP – Customer Master	No selection needed
CPYCYCL – Billing Cycles Master	No selection needed
CPYDHED - Driver Log Headers	DHDATE ge 20030701
CPYDLOG – Driver Log Details	DLDATE ge 20030701
CPYDPCH – Dispatch Details	DPDATE ge 20030701 or eq 0
CPYGL – General Ledger posting	No selection needed
CPYMTRL – Material Master	No selection needed
CPYNOTE – Notes	NDATE ge 20030701
CPYPLST – Price Lists	No selection needed
CPYPRTY – Priority Codes Master	No selection needed
CPYRCST – Route Cost Detail	RCDATE ge 20030701
CPYSALE – Sales File	SDATE ge 20030701
CPYSALEME – Sales File	SDATE ge 20030701
CPYSIGNON – AS400-1 users	No Selection needed
CPYUMES – Unit of Measure Master	No selection needed
CPYVEHC – Vehicle Master File (TMT)	No selection needed
CPYWO1 – Work Order Headers	WOADAT ge 20030701
CPYWO2 – Work Order Detail	WDDATE ge 20030701
CPYXNOTE – 'X' Notes	XNOTE eq 'X'
	NDATE ge 20030701

Record Selection for the Line of Business Data Mart Builds

SALESLIB:

```
BLDALLLAS
        STAX        NE    'T'
        YRMTH       EQ    YRMTHLAS
        STOT        NE    0

BLDALL1PM:
        YRMTH       EQ    YRMTH1PM
        STOT        NE    0
        STAX        NE    'T'

BLDBINSLAS:
        RLFLCODE    LIST  'RL' 'FL'
        CCYCLE      NLIKE 'V%'
        BBILL$      NE    0

BLDBINS1PM:
        RLFLCODE    LIST  'RL' 'FL'
        CCYCLE      NLIKE 'V%'
        BBILL$      NE    0

BLDCORPACT:
        YRMTH       GE    307
        STOT        NE    0
        PRICECODELIST     'H1' 'H2'
        STAX        NE    'T'

BLDFINRES
        CRES        EQ    'Y'
        RESCODE     NE    '*'
        YRMTH       GE    307
        STOT        NE    0

BLDLOSTCUS:
        SDATE       GE    20030701
        STAX        NE    'T'
        CSTOP       GT    0
        XCYCLE      EQ    'X'
        STOT        GT    0

BLDMISSESH
        DPPRTY      EQ    'M'
```

BLDNEWCUST
    CSTRDT   GE   20030701
    STOT   NE   0
    STAX   NE   'T'

BLDPLSTCUS
    SWO#   GT   0
    CPLIST   NE   'NONE'
    STAX   NE   'T'
    SDATE   GE   20030701
    STOT   NE   0

BLDRES
    CRES   EQ   'Y'
    RESCODE NE   '*'
    SDATE   GE   20030701

BLDRO   SWO#   GT   0
    BUSTYPE EQ   'RO'
    STAX   NE   'T'
    SDATE   GE   20030701
    STOT   NE   0

BLDSALE4GL
    YRMTH   GE   0307
    STOT   NE   0

Preparing the Data Warehouse Each Day

Two processes run each day to update work order data.

CPYDAY_01 (Qbatch1)		
Library/Query	**Files Used**	**File Created**
DWLIB/CPYWEEK01	WO1	PRWO1
DWLIB/CPYWEEK02	WO2	PRWO2
DWLIB/CPYWEEK04	DPCH	PRDPCH

Preparing the Data Warehouse Each Week

A number of processes must be run each week to update information for the missed stops query (LDMISSESH). Query CPYWEEK01/DWWEEKLIB must be run first. This query copies RCST, DPCH, CUST, NOTE, SALE, CPRH, and CPRD to the data warehouse data library. It then runs a query to build a missed stop file for load to Qport Access. The file is built from only work order file header records. (Use LDMISSESHD if you want counts and the first line of comments.)

CPYWEEK_01 (Qbatch)		
Library/Query	**Files Used**	**File Created**
DWLIB/CPYWEEK03	RCST	PRRCST
DWLIB/CPYWEEK05	CUST	PRCUST
DWLIB/BLDWEEK07	PRWO1, PRRCST, PRDPCH, MRKTXREF, IQDATE	PRMISSESUM
DWLIB/CPYWEEK08	NOTE	PRNOTE
DWLIB/CPYWEEK09	SALE	PRSALE
PERZIP4/BLDPERZIP4	PRCUST, PRCOMP01, MRKTXREF	PERZIP4WRK
DWLIB/CPYWEEK10	CPRH	PRCPRH
DWLIB/CPYWEEK11	CPRD	PRCPRD

Preparing the Data Warehouse Each Month End

Certain procedures must be run each month end to transfer data to the data warehouse. The processes described below are currently run by the IT department.

Sales Data Mart Processes

1. A file named RUNDATE in library SPTEST on the data warehouse System i contains the month end dates for the LAS (last) month and (1PM) the first prior month. These dates must be incremented by one month to reflect new dates. Use WRKDBF to update this file.
2. Query CPYBCDE in library SALESLIB on the data warehouse System i must be run to begin copying data from the month just closed to the warehouse. CPYBCDE then calls a series of copy processes to copy data from production files needed to build the sales data mart.
3. Query BLDALLCUST in library SALESLIB on the data warehouse System i must be run to build extract files for the sales data mart operational data store. BLDALLCUST in turn calls an additional 37 build processes to create files loaded into Qport Access.

The data warehouse is now ready for sales data mart Qport Access "LDXXXXX" processes in library SALESLIB.

Fixed Asset Data Mart Processes

The five fixed asset queries run at the end of the sales copies. The build (BLDFAKMHRD) runs at the end of the sales builds.

Repair Orders Data Mart Processes

Query CPYCODEKEY in ROLIB on the data warehouse System i must be run after TMT month end close to copy the code key information. It calls the following queries to complete the copy process for the repair order data mart:

CPYCODEKEY - copies certain embedded code descriptions
CPYLBRCHGS - copies RO labor records
CPYPTCHGHS - copies RO part records
CPYROBODHS - copies RO body records
CPYROHDRHS - copies RO header history records

Vehicle Unit Cost Analysis Data Mart Processes

Query CPYMKTSHOP in library VECHLIB runs at the end of the repair order copies.

Route Productivity and Profitability Data Mart Processes

The previous week's productivity and productivity data can be copied to the data warehouse System i each Wednesday. (It is a menu option).
Data are also copied at each month end.

TMT Truck Cost and Utilization Data Mart Processes

Files TT350F, TMT354F, VHCMSTHST, and TMTCODES are copied to DWDATA on the data warehouse System i at month end. The queries in DWLIB and VEHCLIB (TMTMAINT, TMT364Q, TMT364QCUR, TMT913Q, and VEHDATA) described above may then be run using Qport Access.

Glossary

Active listening
giving undivided attention to a speaker in a genuine effort to understand the speakers point of view.

Business intelligence
a generic term for the set of metrics used to analyze business performance at the strategic level within the business.

Business models
a representation, often graphic, of some aspect of a business.

Business rules
a set of rules that defines the explicit operational activities of a company.

Critical success factor
a definable event, condition, or metric that is critical to the success of a business.

Data cleansing
correcting errors and inconsistencies in data to increase accuracy so that the data can be used in a standard company-wide format.

Data elements
the field level elements in the hierarchy of data.

Data mart
a subset of warehoused data – usually specific to one purpose such as sales, inventory, customers, etc.

Data quality audit
a structured survey of files for accuracy and completeness.

Data storage hierarchy
levels of data stored in a computer file: bits, bytes (characters), fields, records, files, and databases.

Data warehouse
the place where warehoused data are kept.

Data warehousing
an approach to organize and store transactional data with the associated master data.

Data workers
people, such as secretaries or bookkeepers, who process the organizations paperwork.

Denormalizing data	process of taking normalized data and bringing it back to first normal form.
Drill-down	the ability to see increasing levels of detail of data without having to rerun the query.
Executive information system	a set of tools used by executives to analyze data needed for decision making.
Extract (Copy)	a data warehousing term for copying legacy system information to a data warehouse staging area.
Flat files	files that are designed with a non-relational architecture.
Foreign key	a field in a record that contains the key, or partial key, to another file.
Joining files	a relational database term used to describe the merging of fields from multiple files into one record format based upon matching key data elements.
Kantor's law	"Everything can look like a failure while you're in the middle." This quote is attributed to Elizabeth Kantor.
Key performance indicator	an important metric used to measure success or failure of a key business function.
Knowledge workers	people, such as engineers or architects, who design products or services and create knowledge for the organization.
Legacy system	a major application system designed to capture the transactions of a business.
Load	a data warehousing term for making data warehouse information available to its users.
Master files	files containing records with information further describing transactions.

Meta data	information about data. Meta data is typically used to assign English-like names for display in a data warehouse environment.
Milestone	a significant point or event in a project.
Milestone schedule	a summary-levels schedule that identifies the milestones of a project.
Normalizing data	the process of removing redundancy in data. A brief discussion of data normalization can found at http://support.microsoft.com/kb/283878.
Online analytical processing	OLAP – tools used with databases to facilitate decision making.
Operational action	implementation activity to accomplish defined tactics and strategy.
Operational data store	the data warehousing environment where changes to operational data are immediately made available to the data warehouse user.
Primary key	the attributes used to establish a unique key for a record.
Project management	the planning, organizing, directing, and controlling of company resources for a relatively short-term objective that has been established to complete specific goals and objectives. (Kerzner)
Project milestone	identifier of a key event in the life of a project.
Query	a generic term for ad hoc reporting tools that allow users to access files.
Qport Access	ad-hoc reporting tool product from New Generation Software, Inc.
Qport SmartView	OLAP engine for the ad-hoc reporting tool product from New Generation Software, Inc.
Record format	the arrangement of fields in a record.
Record key	an identifier in a record.

Record filter	a constraint that limits the selection of records.
Relational files	the architecture using two or more files relating to each other through common keys.
Request for proposal	a document used to identify a set of system requirements for vendor response.
Statement of Work	a document that serves as a formal contract between a project manager, project sponsor and the customer to define the scope of a project.
Strategic action	an action a company defines to attain one or more of its goals.
Structured query language (SQL)	the primary data definition and manipulation language used with most relational database packages.
Systems development life cycle	SDLC – a methodology to manage the design of a system.
Tactical action	an action a company defines to accomplish a strategic action.
Three-dimensional view	a view of information allowing X, Y, and Z dimensions; typically illustrated by a cube.
Transaction files	files containing records identifying discrete events occurring at the lowest level of detail within an application system.
Transform (Build)	the data warehousing term for restructuring and cleansing information in a data warehouse.
Two-dimensional view	a view of information restricted to X and Y dimensions.

Recommended Reading

In addition to the bibliography references, the author has found the following reading materials to be valuable in understanding the business environment:

The E-Myth Revisited, by Michael Gerber, HarperCollins Publishers, 1995, ISBN: 0887307280

The Fifth Discipline: The Art and Practice of the Learning Organization, by Peter M. Singe, Doubleday, 1990, ISBN: 0385260954

The 21 Indispensable Qualities of a Leader: Becoming the Person Others Will Want to Follow, by John C. Maxwell, Thompson Nelson Publishers, 1999, ISBN: 0785274405

Fundamentals of the CIO Role, *CIO Magazine*, the CIO store, 2003

Business @ the Speed of Thought: Succeeding in the Digital Economy, by Bill Gates, Warner Books, 1st edition, 2000, ISBN: 0446675962

The Dilbert Principle: A Cubicle's-Eye View of Bosses, Meetings, Management Fads & Other Workplace Afflictions, by Scott Adams, Harper Business, 1997, ISBN: 0887308589

A Guide to the CMM$^©$: Understanding the Capability Maturity Model$^©$ for Software, by Kenneth M. Dymond, Process Transition, International, Inc., 1998, ISBN: 0964600803

Bibliography

Beck, K. (2000). *Extreme programming explained: Embrace change.* Reading, MA: Addison-Wesley, Inc.

Brown, C., & Topi, H. (2000). *IS management handbook.* 7th ed. Boca Raton, FL: Auerbach Publications.

Foshay, N. (2005). *The influence of end-user metadata on user attitudes toward, and use of, a data warehouse.* Information Integrated Solutions, December 2005.

Hammer, M., Champy, J, (2001), *Reengineering the Corporation: A Manifesto for Business Revolution.* New York, NY: HarperCollins Publishers, 2001

Hill, C., & Jones. G., (2001). *Strategic management theory: An integrated approach.* Boston, MA: Houghton Mifflin Company.

Holmes, A. (2006). Maine's Medicaid Mistakes. *CIO Magazine*, April 15, 2006, 46-54.

Hutchinson, S., & Sawyer, S. (2000). *Computers, communications, and information: A user's introduction, comprehensive version.* 7th ed. Boston: The McGraw-Hill Companies, Inc.

Kachur, K. (2000). *Data warehouse management handbook.* Paramus, NJ: Prentice Hall Press.

Kerzner, H. (2001). *Project management: A systems approach to planning, scheduling, and controlling.* 7th ed. New York: John Wiley & Sons, Inc.

Kimball, R., Reeves, L., Ross, M., Thornthwaite, W., (1998). *The data warehouse lifecycle tToolkit.,* John Wiley & Sons.

Kliem, R., Ludin, I., & Robertson, K. (1997). *Project management methodology: A practical guide for the next millennium.* New York: Marcel Dekker, Inc.

Knowles, M. (1988). *The modern practice of adult education: from pedagogy to andragogy.* Cambridge Book Company

Law, R. (2003). *Principles of Adult Learning.* February 21st issue DM Direct Newsletter.

Laudon, F., & Laudon, J. (2002). *Management information systems: Managing the digital firm.* Upper Saddle River, NJ: Prentice-Hall Inc.

McConnell, S. (1998). *Software project survival: How to make sure your first important project is not your last.* Redmond, WA: Microsoft Press.

Project Management Institute. (2000). *A guide to the project management body of knowledge (PMBOK® Guide).* Sylva, NC: PMI Publishing Division.

Simon, A. (1997). *Data warehousing for dummies.* Foster City, CA., IDG Books Worldwide.

Sobel, M. (1994). *The 12-hour MBA Program.* Paramus, NJ: Prentice Hall

Vella, J. (2002). Learning to listen, learning to teach: The power of dialogue in educating adults. San Francisco, CA: Jossey-Bass.

Zemke, R., & Zemke, S. (1988). 30 Things We Know for Sure About Adult Learning. *Training*, July 1988, 57.

About the Author

 Bruce R. Ullrey is the Chief Information Officer for Rumpke Consolidated Companies – a $350,000,000 regional waste hauling company headquartered in Cincinnati, Ohio. Mr. Ullrey began his career with IBM in 1966 and spent time developing integrated cost estimating systems at the IBM manufacturing facility in San Jose, California. Ullrey has been successfully provisioning and managing IBM mainframe and midrange technology for businesses since 1981. He holds a Masters Degree in Management of Technology and teaches at the university level in the Cincinnati area.

For assistance or answers to any questions regarding Rumpke's data warehouse implementation effort, please feel free to contact the author by e-mail:

Bruce R. Ullrey, MS, CIO
brullrey@rumpke.com

Printed in the United States
90455LV00006B/55/A